MW00719445

To Billy Peters
With Best Wishes

Harvey E. Hann
Aug. 18, 2006

Second edition Printing

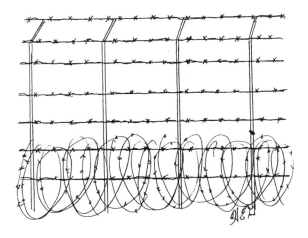

ESCAPE I MUST!

World War II Prisoner of War in Germany

by
Harvey E. Gann

Foreword by
Thomas D. Blackwell
and Mace B. Thurman, Jr.

Introduction by
Charles M. Lowe
and George Phifer

Editor
Betty Wilke Cox

Publisher
Woodburner Press
Austin, Texas

Copyright © 1995 by Harvey E. Gann

All rights reserved. No part of this book may be produced or utilized in any form or by any means, including photocopying, recording or by any information storage and retrieval system without permission in writing from both the Author and the Publisher. Inquiries should be addressed to Woodburner Press, P.O. Box 3927, Austin, TX 78764.

Publisher's Cataloging-in-Publication
(Prepared by Woodburner Press)

Gann, Harvey Elwood, 1920-
Escape I Must! World War II Prisoner of War in Germany / by Harvey E. Gann. Edited by Betty Wilke Cox. 1st edition.
     p.   cm.
    Includes chronology, glossary, index.
    Illus., drawings, maps, photos.
    ISBN 0-9643126-1-1
    1. World War, 1939-1945 - Prisoners and prisons, German.
    2. Prisoners of war - Personal narratives. I. Title.
    940.54´72   95-60566

First edition May 1995
Second edition January 2002

Published by Woodburner Press
P.O. Box 3927
Austin, TX 78764

Printed in the United States of America
Typesetter: Morgan Printing
Printer: Powell Offset Service, Inc.
Binder: Custom Bookbinders

DEDICATED

To those who have stood
so forlornly behind
the barbed wire of the enemy:
Trusting to their own
will to survive,
confident in the courage of
country and comrades,
never doubting the
victory to follow.

To all the mothers, fathers,
family members and friends
who so long anxiously awaited
some word and the return
of their loved ones.

Last but not least
to my lovely wife, Evelyn,
standing tall, ever supportive
and caring throughout my career
and
many trying times.

God bless America.

Table of Contents

Foreword

by Thomas Blackwell

Half a century has passed since courageous American troops scrambled over the beaches at Anzio and Normandy, covered and supported by airplanes operated by valiant airmen. Many of the participants have gone to higher glory, and memory dims for those veterans still alive.

It is important that their heroic deeds not be forgotten, but that they become enshrined in our national heritage. With this in mind, former Technical Sergeant Harvey E. Gann, with the United States Army Air Force during World War II, has been prevailed upon to recount for posterity the stirring saga of his capture and his four escapes as a German prisoner of war.

His thrilling true-life adventure is more riveting than any war story from the great Jack Higgins, Ken Follett, W.E.B. Griffin and others.

I have personally known Harvey Gann since his return from overseas. As prosecutor and judge in Travis County I worked closely with Major Gann during his thirty-eight years with the Austin Police Department. His ability, courage, and talent as a police officer mirror the dedication and determination that enabled him to escape from the German prisoner of war camps.

All Americans can be extremely pleased that Harvey Gann has reduced his memorable adventure to writing.

Thomas D. Blackwell
Brigadier General
U.S. Army N.G. (Ret.)

by Mace B. Thurman, Jr.

Escape I Must! is an interesting and exciting story that will renew your faith in our American culture and social values. I have known the author, Harvey E. Gann, for fifty years, both personally and in the field of criminal jurisprudence. I have learned to respect him for his courage and for his devotion to his country, his community, and his career in law enforcement.

Bomber flights, fights and crashes—four escapes, cloak-and-dagger suspense—comradeship, friendship and trust—are all entangled in an experience told in a simple and forceful manner that will keep your interest throughout the book.

This inspiring tale of a true American hero will instill a sense of pride and patriotism in all who read it.

Mace B. Thurman, Jr.
Senior District Judge
State of Texas

Author's Preface

In the pre-dawn hours of January 30, 1944 our squadron took off for a bombing raid against a large German Luftwaffe fighter base located at the northern tip of the Adriatic Sea. Our briefing officers had warned us that the enemy base was well protected by anti-aircraft emplacements and was home to a large number of Me-109s, one of the best fighter planes in the German Air Force.

Our B-24 Liberator bomber took heavy hits. I was in the top machine-gun turret—my goggles smashed, my nose bloody. Our pilot and co-pilot signaled me to jump. As I bailed out they were right behind me. They never made it. The plane, on fire and riddled by enemy fighters, blew up. Nine men perished. I was the only survivor of our ten-man crew.

I came down on dry land at the edge of the Adriatic Sea. I had barely hauled in my chute before I was captured by German soldiers. I spent the next fifteen months as a prisoner of war.

After being taken as a prisoner I managed to escape three times. Each time I was recaptured.

My fourth attempt was successful. I was free, but not yet out of danger. The war in Europe was almost over. German military and civilian populations alike were on the move or milling about in confusion, seeking to evade or to reach advancing armies of liberation. The cities and countryside were devastated. People were hungry, and many died from lack of medical attention.

I hid wherever I could to avoid detection, slept when I dared, and ate whatever I could find. Managing to cross through the German eastern frontier, I wound up in Odessa, the Ukrainian port on the Black Sea. I finally linked up with American personnel and returned to the United States one day before the war ended in Europe.

My experiences, while unique to me, at the same time mirror many of the trials and privations common to all POWs in the European theater during World War II.

Each year more veterans of that terrible conflict answer their Final Taps. Fewer and fewer of us are left to pass on our stories.

In reaching the decision to write this account of my own experiences, I have tried to recall as accurately as possible the names, places, and sequence of events. I hope my recounting of the details will be of interest to you, the reader.

I must add that I deeply regret what I judge to be my inability to describe adequately the excitement, fear, frustrations, despair, and all the other emotions one feels in situations such as I found myself. I hope that by reading my limited effort and using your imagination—or recalling your own military service— you can share more fully in my experiences.

Now come join me as I get on with my story.

Harvey E. Gann

Acknowledgments

I wish to take this opportunity to thank and to give credit to a number of people, without whose constant urging and unflagging encouragement I could never have written this account of my experiences as a prisoner of war in Germany during World War II.

The most insistent person, almost to the point of demanding, was my dear wife, Evelyn. It was her contention that time was slipping by and that I should put something in print for the sake of our grandchildren at least. Our two daughters, Sandra Allen and Deborah Ledesma, sided with their mother, arguing that all I needed to do was to get started. If I was too contrary to write something, they said, then I should make a voice recording.

My good friends—including Bernie and LaVerne Larson, Rodney and Eleanor Montford, Fred and Janet Owen, George and Johnnie B. Phifer, Richard and Bobbie Schenck, and Allen and Carolyn Steves—added their persuasion and encouragement. Reluctantly I made a tape recording and as I talked, memories I had thought were long lost began flooding back to me. This started the ball rolling. When LaVerne Larson insisted on transcribing the recording on her word processor, I gratefully agreed. She spent a great deal of time on this effort. When she finished I had a paper print-out with which I could further develop the story.

I thank my friends and former neighbors from Del Valle, Texas who responded and shared so generously with reminders of "the good old days."

I want to thank Greg Hatton, author of *Stories My Father Never Told Me.* This account of other POW experiences as well as correspondence with Hatton helped me bring my own project into sharper focus.

I thank Chuck LaMarca and Bob Rector who helped me remember names and dates. As far as I know, we three are the last of our determined band of escapees.

I thank Judge Thomas D. Blackwell, Judge Mace B. Thurman, Colonel Charles M. Lowe, and former Assistant Police Chief George Phifer for reading this book in manuscript and offering their suggestions and corrections. I owe additional thanks to Colonel Lowe—it was he who encouraged me to join the Capital City (Austin, Texas) chapter of the American Ex-Prisoners of War, of which I am a life member.

I thank our good friends, Gene and Mary Jo Powell, owners of Powell Offset Service, Inc., for turning my manuscript into a printed book.

I want to thank my editor, Betty Wilke Cox. It was with her expertise, guidance, and research that my story was organized and developed into a book which I hope you will find worthy of the time you spend in reading it. I also thank Judith Morgan Blackwell, who assisted Ms. Cox with typing, research, and illustrations.

Finally, I hope that my story will encourage and influence other American veterans to preserve their experiences in writing for the benefit of their grandchildren and future generations to read and learn what it really was like when Grandpa was in the Big War.

Introduction

by Charles M. Lowe

Harvey E. Gann has captured in his book what it was like to grow up in rural America during the late 1930s and the last days of the Great Depression, to go into combat in World War II, and to return to a changed post-war society.

He carries you through that period of time when America was an isolationist country that didn't want to become involved in another European war. Isolationism began to thaw somewhat with the build-up of the German and Japanese war machines and the announced Fascist goal of world domination.

The major change came after the "day that will live in infamy," December 7, 1941. The single national purpose became putting an end forever to the totalitarian nations and their threat to free people everywhere.

Patriotism in America didn't just flourish—it raged. This was the impetus for the country to build up an armed force second to none and the industrial base to provide the war materials needed to prosecute war on a global basis.

Harvey Gann has shown how a person coming from a non-violent environment can become an accomplished bomber crew member. As one of a ten-man crew he flew combat missions over enemy-held territory. I speak from experience when I say the most terrifying time on a bomber mission is from the time that you start the bomb run until "bombs away." These minutes are sheer hell.

The second concern for a combat crew member is the bail-out alarm. The parachute jump from a miles-high damaged or burning plane is likely to be an airman's first. No training has prepared him for the jump. If he survives the jump and the landing, his next immediate problem is avoiding capture. He could get lucky and make contact right away with the friendly underground. If he is captured, he hopes he will be taken as a prisoner of war by enemy soldiers. If enemy civilians capture him, he may not live to be turned over to military authorities.

Gann takes the reader from his rural youth, his Army Air Force training, his combat missions, his bail-out, capture and POW experiences, to his four desperate attempts to escape and rejoin American forces.

If you are a combat veteran you will be able to relate to his story. If not, you will experience it vicariously. After reading *Escape I Must!* you will have a better understanding of how people can rise to the circumstances and achieve feats they would never have imagined possible.

Charles M. Lowe
Lt. Col. USAF (Ret.)

by George Phifer

Escape I Must! is a fascinating story that you will enjoy. It is more than the story of a young man who finds himself taken prisoner of war during World War II. It is a story of ingenuity and perseverance during adversity.

As a young airman, Harvey E. Gann cut his way through the barbed-wire fences surrounding *Stalag Luft* VI with a pair of wirecutters made from a door hinge. He and his fellow escapees made their way through the German-held countryside. The escapees were from different parts of the country and each had something unique to contribute as they found their way through the maze of war-torn Europe.

You will be captivated by the courage and daring they displayed.

Gann escaped four times and was recaptured three times. He is one of many POWs who were forced to take part in the Run Up the Road and the Black March. But the story that evolves also tells of the kindness of the average country dweller as the escaped airmen passed through various areas on their way to freedom. Many were willing to help the airmen even at risk to themselves.

In the spring of 1945 the Russians were advancing, the Germans were retreating, and terrified homeless civilians were fleeing in first one direction then another. Yet Gann persisted until he was at last able to rejoin American forces in Odessa, Ukraine on the Eastern Front.

He was returned to the United States on May 7, 1945, the day before the war ended in Europe. After a period of rest and recovery he began his law enforcement career. I was one of his co-workers and friends as we served together in the Austin Police Department.

As you read this suspenseful and humorous account of his experiences you will have a sense that Harvey Gann was put on this earth to accomplish a mission greater than the bombing runs he and the crew of his B-24 Liberator made over southern Europe. This is a book worth reading and one that will make you proud of all the men and women who serve in our armed forces.

George Phifer,
Assistant Chief of Police (Ret.)

SUCKER BOY

I was inducted into the U.S. Army Air Force on September 14, 1942.

I wasn't a pilot—I'd never even been a passenger on a plane. The closest I'd come to the wild blue yonder was an essay I'd written in school: I said I wanted to be an aviator when I grew up. When I pictured the freedom of the open skies, I never imagined I'd have to bail out of a burning plane to save my life or that I would spend fifteen months as a prisoner of war in Germany.

Our family moved to Texas when I was four or five years old. By the time I was six or seven we were living in Del Valle, a rural Travis County farming community seven miles southeast of the capital city, Austin. I suppose the original Spaniards pronounced the name differently but we said "Valley."

Del Valle sprawled out around the crossroads of Colton Road and the old Bastrop Road. Maybe a hundred people lived there when I was growing up in the Thirties. There were a few big, old Victorian-style homes but most people didn't live very grandly during the Depression.

(Photo by Rodney Montford)

The thriving little community of Del Valle as it appeared in 1937.

Many families used windmills for water. Our house got water from a large tank located across the road in the cotton gin yard. Although we had running water in the house, we didn't have indoor plumbing. We used a two-seater outdoor privy at the rear of the house.

For the first few years we used kerosene lamps for light but when the electric power lines came through Del Valle, I remember Dad wired our house. Each room had a single wire dropped down from the ceiling with an attached socket, switch, and bulb.

My mother, Mattie Beatrice, stayed home and took care of the family. For the first few years we lived there, Mother cooked on a wood-burning stove.

I remember when we got the first kerosene (coal oil) stove, called Green Mountain. Mother was thrilled to get it and enjoyed cooking on it. And boy, for a while we ate our favorite pies—chocolate or pineapple—nearly every day.

Our house was a small single-wall frame structure consisting of four rooms—a living room, two bedrooms, and the kitchen. We rented the house and the black-smith shop from Modena Givens Ross. Mrs. Ross was the granddaughter of William Givens from Kentucky who had helped settle the area back in the late 1800s. As more settlers came into the community, William Givens built a store and hauled supplies from Austin in a mule-drawn wagon. Until the Montopolis Bridge was built, Givens had to ford the Colorado River at a shallow crossing. When the Del Valle post office opened in 1878, Givens became the first postmaster.

All of that was way before our time. When we lived in Del Valle there were two stores: Jim Johnson's grocery store and post office, and Clarence Burch's mercantile store and justice of the peace office. The cotton gin was across the road. Lyman Fincher had an ice cream parlor that ran pretty much on the honor system, as I remember. Bob Shelly owned a private telephone exchange and different families ran it from time to time.

My father, William A. Gann, was a blacksmith. There were still mule- or horse-drawn wagons in those days. Dad made or repaired wagon wheels and fitted horse shoes.

When I was old enough I helped in the blacksmith shop after school tending the fire, operating the bellows or running errands. Hanging around the blacksmith shop I got into the habit of picking up metal scraps or broken things and trying to figure something useful I could make out of them.

The shop was open—front and back—and wide enough for wagons to drive inside. Grownups and kids liked to gather there and stand around watching Dad work. He wore a leather apron for protection; cloth could catch a spark and ignite too easily. He'd heat a horseshoe or some other object in the forge till it was hot enough. Then he'd hammer it into shape on the anvil. Sometimes, when he'd be pounding away on a piece of red-hot iron, he'd add something that made the sparks fly like the Fourth of July. Folks yelled and jumped back real quick but they enjoyed the free show.

There were lots of blacksmiths back in the Thirties but Dad's was the only blacksmith shop in Del Valle. He took care of all the farmers' wagon repairs and plow sharpening and such. Instead of paying Dad in cash, the farmers often traded fresh butter and eggs for work done.

My brother, Fred Willard, was two years younger than I was. We enjoyed the freedom that goes with living in a rural community. If we were poor we hardly knew it—nobody had much money in those days. Nobody we knew anyway.

I was late starting to school. Mother said it seemed like every September, when it came time for me to enroll in the first grade, I came down with a different childhood disease. By the time I was finally well enough to go to school I was running years behind my age group. At the time I couldn't see any particular advantage to all my fevers, sore throats, swellings, bumps, and rashes. But I guess in the long run I acquired a certain amount of immunity to diseases—I'd already had them all. I grew up to be a pretty healthy adult and that certainly came in handy later.

We kids used to call the place "Dull Valle" because we thought there was never anything exciting to do. Now, looking back more than half a century, I realize we had fun. We used to play hide-and-seek around the cotton gin yard and "ride" the bales. Sometimes we'd listen in on the party line while some young lady was being courted over the telephone by her beau—but usually our giggling gave us away.

Willard and I used to go fishing in Onion Creek or the Colorado River with our cane poles, using worms or grasshoppers for bait. Our Dad was always ready to close the blacksmith shop and head for the river. He considered fishing to be time well spent. A mess of fresh fish made a fine Sunday dinner for us and any company we might have.

Most of the time my brother and I took our .22 rifle along and hunted squirrels in the pecan trees along the bottomland. I still have the single-shot Winchester bolt-action .22-caliber rifle that we used. I remember Dad bought it for us as a Christmas gift and, at the time, it cost about $5.25 at A. D. Waterson's General Store in nearby Creedmoor. Creedmoor was nearly twice the size of Del Valle and had more stores.

Cotton was the main crop of most of the farms in the community. The rich, black soil around Del Valle was some of the best in the state and well suited to it. Cotton was cultivated and picked by hand. Work in the fields was seasonal. Blacks who did most of the farm work stayed in small tenant houses provided for migrant workers. Willard and I knew most of the black families because their parents brought blacksmith work to Dad's shop. We played and fought with them just like any other kids. If there were any racial feelings, we were not aware of them.

The cotton gin across the road from our house was the biggest business around so, when I was old enough, that's where I went to work.

My first big job didn't have an impressive title. I was a "sucker boy" for the Del Valle cotton gin. I was responsible for unloading the seed cotton from the wagons. The "sucker" was a large vacuum tube about twelve or fourteen inches in diameter. The tube sucked the cotton up from the wagon and took it through the gin stands where the cotton lint was separated from the seeds. I could truthfully brag that mine was the most important job in the whole gin. After all, if the cotton didn't get sucked up into the stand it couldn't be ginned. Right?

I remember a scary incident when I was about fifteen years old. In June 1935, our family had been visiting friends in Lexington. This was a town in Lee County about forty-five miles east of Austin. Lexington was a little bitty place but it was still about five times bigger than Del Valle. Our friends lived outside town on a small farm and we went to their house on a Friday afternoon.

Rain came down almost constantly while we were there. When we started home on Sunday afternoon it seemed as if the whole country was under water. Our 1932 Studebaker was able to get us through all the muddy roads and high water until we got almost to Austin. Then we learned that the Montopolis Bridge over the Colorado River on the east side of town was washed out. We had to go into Austin and cross the Congress Avenue Bridge. Even then we had to wait for several hours for the water to go down. Our usual one-hour trip from Lexington to our home at Del Valle lasted until almost midnight. We felt lucky to get home at all.

I went as far as I could in the Colorado School (named for the Colorado River). Ours was a small, two-room school with the first four grades in one room and the last grades in the other. There were two other schools, one for Mexicans and one for blacks. That was the custom in Texas at the time and I guess none of us thought much about it.

There wasn't a local high school back then, not until 1958 or '59—and by then the Del Valle community I had grown up in was only a memory. When we youngsters reached high school age we rode into Austin on the bus from Garfield, a small community southeast of Del Valle. Bigger and older than most of my classmates, I graduated from Austin High School in 1941.

One unseasonably warm Sunday afternoon in early December I was visiting the home of some of my friends. One of the boys was outside listening to music on his car radio when suddenly an announcer interrupted the program. The boy burst into the house and called us all to come hear the news for ourselves.

We turned the car radio up full blast and crowded around, listening to the first report that the Japanese had bombed Pearl Harbor.

The next day President Franklin D. Roosevelt addressed the nation on radio and made it official.

We were at war.

Representatives of the Army Air Force had been scouting around for a good location to establish a base. They kept coming back to look at Del Valle. The relatively high, relatively level area looked good to them.

Finally, in the spring of 1942 the government brought in heavy earth-moving equipment and hired about 1,600 civilians to do the work of transforming 3,000 acres of good cotton land into an airbase. They tore down or removed about thirty houses, the two stores, Dad's blacksmith shop, the school, the chapel, and the telephone exchange. The cotton gin where I'd worked was moved down the road.

One building, the Givens' Round House—so called because it actually was round with no square corners—was spared, remodeled, and used as the noncommissioned officers' club on the base. It later burned to the ground.

As soon as work started on building the airbase, I got a job as a mechanic's helper working on heavy equipment. I worked at this for several days and then I heard that the government needed truck drivers. Several of my friends and I decided we would rather drive dump trucks than do mechanic work on tractors so we immediately changed jobs.

We caught a lowboy trailer to Killeen, Texas and there we picked up our trucks. They were large earth-moving dump trucks with five forward speeds. None of us had ever driven anything other than beat-up old jalopies. I think you could have heard us grinding up gears all the way back to Austin until we got the hang of double-clutching. With a series of forward leaps and jolting stops, we finally got back to Del Valle.

I worked there on the base until I got my notice of induction on September 14, 1942. I reported to Fort Sam Houston in San Antonio. Five days later, September 19, the Del Valle Air Base I'd helped to build was officially activated for use by troop carrier aircraft.

(Photo by Rodney Montford)

The Givens Round House was used as the noncommissioned officers' club on the Del Valle Air Base until the house burned to the ground.

FLY BOY

I remembered my boyhood dream of flying so I requested the Army Air Force.

After induction I was accepted into Airplane Mechanic School at Keesler Field near Biloxi, Mississippi. When I completed training at Keesler, I received a transfer to Willow Run.

On our way from Keesler, our train stopped in Chicago. When we got off the train, we were met by the U.S.O. They held a big dance for us and that really cheered us all up.

Willow Run was the site of a big Ford Motor plant near Detroit, Michigan. I'd been born in Detroit on November 28, 1920 but the family had moved when I was still a baby. I had no memories of the place and no relatives there that I knew of.

The Ford plant used mass-production methods of aircraft assembly, turning out B-24 Liberator bombers as fast as possible. One thing that was of special interest to me while at Willow Run was the opportunity to see the famous aviator, Charles Lindbergh, flying a P-47 over the plant. At least that's what we recruits were told by some of our training personnel and we all believed them.

When I completed this phase of training the Air Force sent me to Aerial Gunnery School at Laredo, Texas.

I enjoyed the school. Much of it consisted of actually firing the .50-caliber machine guns we later would use in combat. For practice we fired from our plane at a target towed by another plane. Sometimes tow planes were flown by WAAFs but I don't know if ours were or not.

The practice firing was more fun than a shooting gallery in a traveling carnival—until one day I got careless.

I was practice firing from the plane's top turret when a red-hot extracted shell casing fell into the top of my loosely laced shoe. I yelled so loud my crew mates must have thought we'd flown into enemy airspace and were under attack. It didn't take me long to climb down from the turret and remove my shoe and the hot metal casing. I still carry a scar from the burn on the inside of my left ankle.

I will say one thing—I learned a valuable lesson: Always lace and tie your shoes properly before firing a machine gun.

Besides gunnery practice we spent quite a bit of time on aircraft identification—German and Japanese as well as British and our own. This was to keep us from shooting down our own or our allies' planes. In combat, you have to make split second decisions to shoot or not to shoot. Some airmen, if they weren't sure, called a plane a B-2. That meant, it'll *be too* bad if it's not friendly.

After we completed our gunnery training we were entitled to wear the Aerial Gunner's Wings on our shirts or jackets. I was proud to be one of a select group to wear those wings. I tried not to let my mind dwell on just how fragile those wings could be or how soon they might be clipped in combat. I guess most of us try to hold on to the idea that bad things only happen to the other guy. I know I didn't expect to trade my gunner's wings for a POW medal.

My next stop after Laredo was Bomber Crew Training at Davis-Monthan Field near Tucson, Arizona. There I realized just how dangerous flying can be. High mountains edged the desert airbase on two sides. A couple of bombers with full crews flew smack into the side of the mountains. We could see where one of them hit and burned.

My next transfer sent me to Blythe, California for further training. Seemed like every base we went to, Kilroy had been there before us. Then I was transferred to Brunning, Nebraska and assigned to a B-24 bomber crew. Ordinarily a bomber crew was composed of ten men. Sometimes an extra man would go along as a photographer.

Ben N. Kendall was the pilot. Richard Pelkey was the co-pilot and Harry B. McGuire was navigator. Pershing J. Hill was bombardier. They were all lieutenants. The rest of us were sergeants. I was flight engineer and top-turret gunner. Gerald W. Harrington was assistant engineer and gunner. Given C. Grooms was radio operator and gunner. Nick Gavales was tailgunner. Charles A. LaMarca was ball-turret gunner and Harold T. Thompson was gunner.

This was the bomber crew that I would fly with in combat, the one—with the exception of Pelkey and LaMarca—that later would be shot out of the sky over Italy.

Our last stop, or staging area, was Kansas City. Our equipment was issued and we were given our shots.

I was twenty-three years old and ready to go overseas.

We were transferred to the staging area at Miami, Florida. On the night of December 14, 1943 we took off for our rendezvous with Fate in the skies over Germany. We flew over in our assigned B-24s. I will never forget how beautiful the city of Miami looked that night with all the bright lights reflected in the sparkling water. All of this added to our realization that we were headed into combat. We were somber with the knowledge some of us wouldn't make it back home.

I must say that the fact we were headed for combat in no way cast a doom-and-gloom attitude on our own crew members or on the four extra ground crew members who were flying with us. I recall that while we were flying we could look down and see the mighty Amazon River as it flowed almost four thousand miles through the jungles of South America. We seemed to be flying for hours over nothing but green forest and river.

About this time our whole flight crew decided to play a joke on one of the ground crew guys. Just because he was in flight operations, he seemed to think he'd have some say-so as to who would be sent out on what target. He'd been having himself a great time telling us how he'd be waiting for us when we came back from our bombing missions. He was pretty full of his own imagined importance.

When we got tired of listening to him boast, several of us quietly talked our pilot, Lt. Kendall, into helping to play a joke on the loudmouth.

Lt. Kendall agreed. We passed the word to everyone but our intended victim. One of our crew managed to hide the victim's chute. Then we all started talking about how awful it would be if we had engine trouble and had to bail out over the jungle or the croc-filled river.

We'd planted the seed of worry in our victim's mind. All we had to do was sit back and wait.

Our pilot's timing was perfect. "We're in trouble," he called back to us. "I'm going to feather the number-two engine." We all looked out the waist-gunner's windows. Sure enough, we saw the feathered engine. Lt. Kendall was carrying realism to the extreme for our little joke.

Then the bail-out alarm sounded. We all scrambled for our chutes and I threw open the escape hatch. We crowded around the open hatch and waited while Sgt. Loudmouth frantically searched for his chute. After what must have seemed like an eternity to him, our pilot called back, "All clear. Everything under control."

We all kept straight faces and never let on we'd set him up. I don't think he ever knew we'd tricked him. I do know that when he finally found his chute he sat on it or carried it around with him the remainder of the trip.

Our course of travel took us down through South America to Fortaleza, Brazil on the Atlantic coast. Brazil had declared war on Germany and Italy in

August 1942 and joined the Allied war effort. Air fields in Brazil made the crossing to Africa and the Mediterranean area a little safer.

I think it was in Fortaleza that Christmas came and went. There was nothing much special about it for us. We had a good dinner on the base and went swimming in the beautiful waters of the Atlantic Ocean. (Brazil, being south of the equator, is warm and sunny in December.) This was my second Christmas away from home and I missed it very much. I know the rest of the group felt the same as I did.

We knew that when we left Fortaleza we would be flying over the ocean for many hours. We didn't feel good about the long flight over water and none of us looked forward to it with pleasure. Adding to our concern was the knowledge that when we landed in Africa we would be subject to enemy action.

We crossed the Atlantic to Dakar at the tip of French West Africa. After a short lay-over at Dakar we proceeded to Marrakesh, North Africa for a few days and then on to the southern tip or boot heel of Italy. The Allies had invaded Sicily in July 1943 and in September Italy had signed an Armistice with us but the Germans still held control of large parts of the country.

We landed at Grottaglie Air Base, Italy, on January 7, 1944. Grottaglie had been the site of Mussolini's Roma dirigible hangars and also a Luftwaffe base before the Allies occupied it in December 1943. The airbase there became the home for the 449th Bombardment Group (the "Flying Horsemen") of the Fifteenth Air Wing. Major General Nathan F. Twining commanded the Fifteenth. General Twining had been the commander of bombing operations in the Pacific

Theater in 1942-43. He took command of the Fifteenth on January 1, 1944. Colonel Darr H. Alkire from San Francisco was combat commander of the 449th.

I remember well the first night we arrived. No barracks or living quarters were ready for us. We didn't even have tents yet. We had to remain on board our B-24 and sleep on top of our gear as best we could. We were only a few miles back from where the American forces had pushed their way up into Italy. We just knew the German Air Force would bomb our base at any moment.

Sometime around midnight we heard the sound of an approaching airplane and then a loud explosion followed by the bursting of shells. We expected our plane on the ground—literally a sitting duck—to be hit next. We'd all die right there without flying a single mission. We didn't sleep much that night.

The next day we learned that a Royal Air Force Mosquito bomber had crashed and burned. The de Haviland "Mozzie," a night fighter and reconnaissance plane as well as a bomber, carried a heavy payload. All the noise and exploding shells we heard came from the ammo on board the Mosquito, exploding as it burned.

This was our introduction to war. We were just a bunch of green young guys in our early twenties who had never been in combat. It scared the pants off us.

The next day we were able to set up our tents in a grove of olive trees fairly close to the runway. I'd heard the expression "sunny Italy," but my memories are of cold rain and mud.

At first we had no means of heating our tents. Our solution was to pour a small amount of gasoline into a dirt-filled can and light this for our source of heat.

This worked pretty well unless you thought the fire was out and you tried to add more gas. The mistake resulted in a big burst of flaming gasoline being thrown everywhere. Usually the tent burned down and we ran for our lives. We learned fast not to add gas to those dirt-filled cans. If you were one of the slow learners, you wound up with nothing left but the underwear you were wearing—or worse.

Grottaglie was a small town, not much more than a village, in a hilly landscape pocked with caves or grottoes. The people there made lots of pottery. The wet, sticky clay may have been great for pots but it made for poor runways. The landing runways consisted of metal lathing over mud.

Bathing was a problem we solved by going into Taranto, a city located inside the heel of Italy about thirty-five kilometers (almost twenty-two miles) from Grottaglie. Taranto had been Italy's largest naval base until the Allies took it in September 1943. The harbor became an important supply line for the Allies. The city was so full of Allied service personnel it hardly seemed we were in a foreign country. We got there about once a week, if we were lucky.

Kilroy was here

COMBAT

At the time we were in Grottaglie, in January 1944, the German Luftwaffe still dominated the skies over most of Europe. A great deal of aerial warfare remained ahead for the Allies and the Air Force didn't waste any time in putting us to work.

Our crew never got around to naming our plane or painting on "nose art"—a picture of a movie star or cartoon character—the way some crews did. We began flying bombing missions within a couple of days of our arrival.

Our Consolidated B-24 Liberator bombers were sometimes called "flying boxcars." They weighed about thirty tons each. It's true they didn't have sleek, trim lines but they had pretty good reputations for dropping their payloads and making it back home. Those big bombers had the longest production run of any American aircraft in World War II.

Your adrenaline really flowed as you'd sit there in your ship at the end of the runway and watch hundreds of planes, their bellies loaded with bombs, take off just minutes ahead of you from those mud-filled and pock-marked strips. You knew someone was bound to mess up. The longer you waited for your green light to signal takeoff the more certain you were that you would be the one.

We usually flew four- to six-hour missions. They were physically and mentally exhausting.

In early 1944 bad weather caused some of the Fifteenth's strategic bombing missions to be scrubbed. But our squadron, the 718th, had already participated in about thirteen or fourteen raids. Most of these raids were over northern Italy and the Balkans where we had lost several ships.

After each bombing raid we always had a de-briefing. Here we recalled as much information as we could so that intelligence would be up-to-date and we would be better informed on our next raids. Details concerning the damage done to the target and the number of enemy planes encountered were all very important, as well as placement of anti-aircraft artillery.

Our own losses of men and the number of planes shot down were confirmed at these de-briefings. One of my crewmen, Charles A. (Chuck) LaMarca, had been shot down January 14, on his fourth mission. LaMarca was flying extra as a photographer on a B-24 named "White Fang" when the plane went down.

I was sorry to lose LaMarca—he was a good man.

In the early morning hours of our fateful day of January 30, 1944 we ate an early breakfast and met in the squadron briefing room. Nine heavy-bomber groups from the Fifteenth, escorted by P-38 Lightnings and some British Spitfires, would fly the mission. We were shown our bombing target and route for that mission on a large map.

It was my fourteenth mission. The target for the day was a German Air Force fighter base located at the northern tip of the Adriatic Sea near the industrial town of Udine, Italy. We were warned that the base was home to a large number of Me-109s, one of the best fighter planes in the German Luftwaffe, and was well protected by anti-aircraft emplacements.

The Messerschmitt Me-109s had been in production since the mid-1930s when the Germans combat-tested them in the Spanish Civil War. They had plenty of time to refine them and eliminate any faults. The single-engine, single-seat plane had become the backbone of the Luftwaffe fighter squadrons all the way from North Africa to Russia.

A combat wing might be fifty-four to sixty-three planes. As well as I can recall, we were to be high squadron at the very rear of the bomber formation. We all recognized this was liable to be a bad day at Blackrock. The odds were against us. Not all of us would be coming back.

Our anxiety level was already high. However, there were no mishaps on the takeoff. Our plane was among the last to taxi into position. We took off in the gray light of dawn. We started using our oxygen at about 10,000 feet. Our electrically-heated suits, as well as heavy flight suits and jackets, were necessary to keep us from freezing at 25,000 feet or more. We all rendezvoused and climbed to our cruising altitude.

We headed for our target. As daylight broke there was not a cloud in the sky. We could see the blue water of the Adriatic Sea beneath us as we made our way north to the target. There was very little talk on the intercom and the flight, so far, was uneventful.

Lt. Fletcher Porter had replaced Lt. Pelkey as co-pilot. Pelkey had been assigned to a different ship. We had a replacement for LaMarca as ball-turret gunner. We gunners test-fired our .50-caliber machine guns with short bursts. We became even more watchful and alert as we approached the fighter base. We were now only a few miles from our target, placing us well within range of German interceptors.

About noon we spotted a large number of Me-109s but they kept their distance from us. To keep from being hit by their own ground fire, the German fighter planes didn't engage bombers while their own anti-aircraft guns were firing at us. Later they swooped in to pick off any of the bombers that might be crippled or damaged.

The German anti-aircraft eighty-eights on the ground started shooting at our formation. You could see the black bursts of smoke from the ack-ack. You could hear and feel the thump of the explosions. You felt you were flying through a dark cloud and you wondered how you had come this far without being hit. The German flack continued all the way up to the target.

Our Norden bombsight held us on course. I remember on the bomb run I looked down through the bomb bays and saw the exploding bombs dropped by our ships ahead of us. I could see several German planes on the ground and several buildings, all of them burning.

Just as we dropped our bomb load, the German fighters began to attack us. Several of them came in from about six o'clock high and some from the three- and nine-o'clock positions.

One of the Me–109 fighters zoomed in at our rear. I suppose all of us gunners were shooting at him. I know as he came in he was underneath my gun's fire stops and I had to stop shooting. As he came by on our left wing I saw his head was rolled over against the side of his cockpit. I felt certain he was dead.

Another fighter came in on our right wing, slightly lower than our plane. As I watched him, he pulled up the nose of his plane and flew directly into the bomb bay of our right wing-man's plane. I thought the German fighter pilot was probably already dead when he rammed the bomber. Both planes plummeted in a burst of flames. It was a terrible sight. I am sure none of the bomber crew lived long enough to bail out.

I noticed our lead plane streaming fire from both right-wing engines. In the brief second I could keep it in sight I saw it peel off to the right of the formation. I feel certain it exploded.

My attention riveted back to a German fighter boring in from about six o'clock high. I started shooting at him. I could see his tracers and cannon fire. I had such a sense of helplessness I prayed to shrivel to about the size of a BB. At that moment a round from his cannon must have hit my gun turret. The explosion tore away part of the Plexiglas. I guess the explosion of the shell caused me to bump my head against the turret. My nose was bleeding. My goggles were broken and I could hardly see.

I felt a sharp, stinging sensation just beneath my neck along my left collarbone. I thought for sure I was mortally wounded but in those tight quarters and in my bulky, electrically-heated "teddy-bear" flight suit I couldn't be sure. I climbed down out of my turret to check myself out. I was greatly relieved to find that only a small fragment of metal or something had barely penetrated my skin. Other than being shook up I was not in any serious condition.

I patted myself down, confirming that I was still alive and in one piece, and climbed back into the turret. I tried to fire again and discovered my guns had been rendered useless. The cannon shell must have damaged the gear ring of the turret. I tried to operate the guns with the manual cranks but they wouldn't work. I'd have risked frostbite to take off my gloves and try to fix the guns. But I could see there was no need—there was nothing I could do. I had barely absorbed this in my shocked and confused mind before I saw fire licking out of a large hole at the rear of the left inboard engine nacelle.

Our number-two engine was in flames. I caught the strong smell of gasoline. I knew if a tracer round or cannon shell hit us the plane would explode.

(Photo by author)

The author used models of a B-24 and a Me–109, made by his friend Lloyd Polk, to recreate an aerial battle.

BAIL OUT!

My guns were not working and our plane was on fire. I hurriedly scrambled down from my turret. I wanted to tell Lt. Kendall I thought we should abandon ship.

As I dropped down from the turret onto the flight deck, I saw that Lt. Kendall and the co-pilot, Lt. Porter, were out of their seats. They both were heading toward the bomb bay catwalk to bail out.

I was in position to enter the bomb bays. I picked up my parachute from the flight deck—the tight quarters and bulky clothing made it difficult for a gunner to wear his chute while in the turret—and secured the fasteners into my chute harness. I stepped down onto the catwalk and motioned to the pilot and co-pilot that I was going to jump. With all the other noises and with my ears still ringing from the explosion in my turret I hadn't heard the pilot sound the bail-out alarm, but when Lt. Kendall nodded in agreement I felt sure he had.

We were still under attack by the Me-109s. I figured the rest of the crew had already jumped or were dead.

My pilot and co-pilot were ready to get out onto the catwalk with me. I gave them a final look and then I jumped.

It was my first jump. I didn't know what to expect but I knew I had to get out of that burning plane. We'd been given lectures on the ground but we had never actually practiced jumping the way airborne troops did. The paratroopers were expected to have to jump—we weren't.

I remembered I was supposed to count to ten but I doubt if I did—certainly not consciously. As soon as I knew I was clear of the ship and wouldn't hang up on the fuselage, I tried to yank the rip-cord. The chute was the chest type and it was attached rather loosely to my body harness. I didn't tug hard enough. The chute didn't open. I reached across my chest with my left arm and smacked my right hand. The jar popped the chute open. There I was hanging in the clear blue sky all by myself, freezing cold and scared to death.

As the chute burst open and filled with air, I was lifted back up by the force. I felt chute-shock, as if I had hit the end of a bungee cord and it had snapped me back. I had the strange sensation that the wind was carrying me up instead of down. Then I was floating. I was still deafened from explosions; for several seconds I couldn't hear any sounds.

After a few more seconds my hearing began to return. I heard the wind whistling in the chute's shroud lines as I was falling. I also heard something I didn't want to hear—the sounds of approaching airplanes. I swiveled around toward the direction of the noise and saw two Me-109s coming toward me. I was afraid they were going to strafe me. I began swinging back and

forth to make myself a
more difficult target. My
rocking caused the chute
to dump some air. That
scared me—I might make
a streamer out of the
chute.

I stopped my swinging
motion and tried to pull
my Colt .45 automatic pistol from my shoulder hol-
ster. I don't know what I
thought I was going to do
with it—a pistol wouldn't
have been much use
against Messerschmitt
machine guns—but my
chute harness and my flying clothes were all so tight
and bulky I couldn't get the gun out.

I prayed, "Good Lord, you have saved me so far.
Please do it again." I just hung there expecting the
German planes to start shooting at my helplessly
dangling body.

The two fighter planes swooped by so close I felt their
slipstream. I could see the pilots, each in his one-man
cockpit. To my surprise and relief the pilots threw me
salutes and flew on their way. Maybe they took pity on
me or maybe they figured I was done for in any case. I
was left hanging there in my chute.

I looked down at the Earth and realized I was out
over the Adriatic Sea. In my haste to put my chute on
before I jumped from our plane I had neglected to don
my "Mae West," a survival flotation device in case you

come down in water. I realized in all probability that is exactly what I was about to do unless I could somehow change my course

I started pulling on shroud lines and maneuvering myself toward the shoreline. I was surprised at how clearly I could see details as I drifted down. I saw a motor launch headed in my direction. I hoped if I hit the water that the launch got to me before I drowned. As I continued to descend, I could tell I was going to land on the ground. With very little wind to throw me off or to help me, I estimated I'd land about three hundred yards in from the water's edge. I tried to spot possible cover or hiding places but the beach was bare for a mile or more.

Just before I hit the ground it seemed the Earth spread out and rushed up to meet me.

The next thing I knew I landed hard on the ground. The chute settled all over me and I felt trapped. I fought my way out of the folds and started gathering my chute in my arms. Part of me reacted with blind instinct for survival. Part of me remembered our instructions: *Hide the chute. Avoid capture.* I ran over to a nearby drainage ditch, discarded the chute, and searched for a place to conceal myself.

The only cover I could see was the line of trees I'd spotted from the air and it was at least a mile away. I started running in that direction. I had hardly covered a hundred yards before I heard voices hollering at me: *Halt!*

CAPTURED

I looked back toward the shore and saw three German soldiers in gray uniforms running in my direction. They were pointing their rifles at me.

Evidently they had been on the motor launch I'd observed as I was coming down in my chute. I'd been unable to see the launch after I landed because of sand dunes between the water and me. I knew it was impossible for me to get away from the soldiers—they had rifles. I stopped, raised my hands in the air, and waited for them to approach me.

One of the soldiers remained about a hundred yards back as a precaution. The other two came up to me with their rifles on the ready. When they were a few feet away from me one of them placed his rifle on the ground, walked up to me, and began trying to search me.

Up close I could see the soldier was very young. I didn't learn until years later that as the war had dragged on the Germans lost so many soldiers the *Führer* forced young boys and elderly men into uniform.

Standing there in what was left intact of my flight gear and with blood on my face I must have been a terrifying sight. It seemed to me my captors were as afraid of me as I was of all three of them.

When the young soldier came to my .45 automatic in the shoulder holster underneath my flight suit, he must have thought it was hot or something because he didn't want to touch it. He acted scared and fumbled around. He had a hard time trying to get it out of my holster. Finally I motioned to him that I would take it out for him. Relieved, he nodded in agreement.

I reached my hand in and pulled my pistol from its holster. As my fingers closed around the grip, desperate thoughts raced through my head. I might be able to shoot one soldier, perhaps even his buddy—but I knew the third soldier, still a good hundred yards away, could drop me with his rifle before I could race for cover.

Good judgment prevailed. I figured as long as I remained alive I had a chance to survive. Reluctantly I surrendered my gun to the frightened young soldier.

After that he completed his search swiftly. He immediately found the compact airmen's escape kit that we all carried. The kit contained a small amount of American money as well as a compass and maps of the general area in which we were operating.

Right from the beginning I could tell my German captors were under the impression that I was a P-38 pilot. They said that I was flying a Lightning and I didn't try to tell them otherwise. Since P-38s were flying escort for us that day I am sure some of them must have been shot down also.

The soldier and his buddy motioned for me to walk toward the motor launch. We waded out to the launch. Several other soldiers waiting in the launch pulled us aboard. They started the motor and drove over to a parachute floating in the water. Tangled in the chute I saw a large piece of metal that I thought might have been part of a plane's catwalk. As they started pulling the chute from the water, I could see a body entangled in the harness and cords.

The soldiers showed little emotion as they dragged the body aboard the boat. I am sure they must have performed the task on previous occasions.

As soon as the soldiers dragged it aboard I recognized the body of Lt. Porter, my co-pilot. I fought to keep all expression from my face and pretended not to recognize the body. At that time I was not certain that our plane had exploded but I feared it had. After seeing my dead co-pilot with his chute tangled around the metal, I felt sure that I was the only member of my crew who had bailed out of the burning plane. The thought of all of them dying in the plane was deeply disturbing, but I managed to show as little emotion as the Germans did.

Later I was to learn from several airmen whose planes had been shot down ahead of me that they saw my chute open almost at the same moment as our plane blew up.

The German soldiers pulled Lt. Porter's body aboard. They then motored to a nearby town where we docked. I was taken ashore and driven by automobile to the soldiers' headquarters. I was placed in a large room where I remained by myself for some time. Eventually my captors brought several other prisoners into the room with me. We exchanged a little information and tried to guess where we were and what would happen to us next.

About that time one of my fellow airmen pointed out a half-inch hole in the collar of my flight suit. Once more I realized how lucky I had been. Not only had I escaped death in the explosion of my plane but I had also barely missed being hit in the neck by a bullet or a large piece of metal.

"If you were a cat," the airman remarked, "you'd still have seven lives to go." I nodded in agreement. When I look back over my past I realize just how much truth there was in his statement.

We prisoners were left huddled together there in the room without too much attention paid to us. The soldiers, however, bustled around busily. Several of them snapped *Heil Hitler!* salutes and clicked their boot heels together in the Nazi style. I guess it was about then it finally soaked in on me that I was a prisoner of war of Germany.

PRISONER OF WAR

L ater in the afternoon our captors brought us some food. I was surprised to realize how many hours it had been since our pre-flight breakfast. The meal consisted of a bowl of soup made of barley or some type of grain, a small wedge of cheese and a slice of black bread. We all ate every crust and crumb, and although it was not enough to fill us, we were very glad to get it.

We were advised by an English-speaking German officer that we would have to remain where we were until the next day. Then trains would take us to Germany.

The rest of the day we sat around and talked to each other. Several of the men were from the same squadron and a few had been crew-mates from the same airships. We talked freely among ourselves. I don't recall suspecting that there might have been a plant or an impostor among us. Anyway, most of the conversation was about how each of us had managed to survive, how we were captured, how our families would react to notice of our being missing in action, and what was going to happen to us next.

I learned later that my parents didn't receive word I was a POW for about two months. Before they knew

I was a captive, I had already made my first attempt at escape.

That night we sacked out on the floor and grabbed what sleep we could when we were not hearing *"Heil Hitler!"* and boot heels.

The next morning the Germans loaded us all into a truck and drove us into town, which was not very far away as I recall Anyway, when we arrived in the town—I think it must have been Verona, Italy—we were dropped off with our guards near the main plaza or square at about noon. We'd been there only a short while before a large group of citizens began to gather around us.

There were about a dozen or fifteen of us POWs. We were all enlisted men—captured officers were processed into separate camps.

The civilians easily identified us as airmen. Those parts of Italy still under control of the Germans had suffered from heavy Allied bombing raids. The civilians were angry and afraid. They began to curse and spit at us. A few tried to get close enough to hit us with their fists or anything else that was handy.

After the war, I found out just how lucky we were. On October 18, 1942 the Germans had issued an order that "terror pilots" who were forced down were to be handed over to local lynch mobs. Only our German guards saved us from hanging. I suspect the guards were motivated more by the need for any intelligence they might force from us than by any sense of mercy or compassion for our lives.

FOR YOU THE WAR IS OVER

While we prisoners were busy trying to fend off the angry Italian civilians, a German officer came up to our guards and instructed them to move us to the train station where we were loaded onto a regular passenger car. One of the first things they told us was: "For you the war is over!"

When we first started our journey, we were not told of our destination in Germany. Later we learned that we were headed for Frankfurt am Main, an industrial city in central Germany.

Our trip from Italy took us up through the Tyrolean Alps by way of the Brenner Pass to Austria. I remember thinking how beautiful the mountains and valleys were—all snow-covered, picture-calendar vistas. I suppose, had I been making the journey under different circumstances, I really would have enjoyed taking in all the spectacular scenery. But at the time I was nearly numb with uncertainty and fear. I hoped I was having a bad dream from which I would awake with no memories to haunt me.

As we continued our journey we began to pass through larger cities. The Germans made no effort to cover the windows from us or to keep us from looking out. We could tell that all of the railroads and train stations along the way had been heavily damaged by Allied bombers.

We began to be afraid that we might happen to be passing through one of the railyards while our own bombers or fighter planes were making a raid.

Our luck remained with us. I can recall only one instance when we were in the railyards in a large city somewhere close to Frankfurt while a British night bombing raid was taking place. We saw great fires burning all over the city. When the raid started our train stopped moving. We remained stationary for an hour or more before we were able to move through the railyards and continue on our way.

If I remember correctly, we arrived in Frankfurt late in the evening of the next day. We were taken to the reception center for Allied airmen. In 1944 most POWs were airmen rather than ground soldiers and the Luftwaffe had control over them. Germans were convinced that airmen who bailed out over Germany were especially trained in terrorism and sabotage so we were guarded closely and kept separate from other POWs.

The reception center, known as *Dulag Luft*, was where the Germans carried out all the interrogations and made assignments to regular POW camps in and around Germany. Our German captors passed out cardboard boxes or suitcases (sometimes called "captive cases") containing personal toilet articles—courtesy of the Red Cross. I kept the Gillette razor and used it for many years after my return to civilian life.

At *Dulag Luft* guards took me to a small room. I was locked up to await I knew not what. I remained there in solitary for three days or more—I lost track of time. The room was about eight by ten feet and had a wooden cot with a straw mattress and one blanket for cover. There were no windows in the room and the only source of light was a small electric bulb screwed into a socket in the middle of the ten-foot high ceiling.

Again, the food consisted of a small bowl of soup for the evening meal. For breakfast they brought a slice of black bread with a thin layer of marmalade smeared across it and a tin cup of ersatz coffee. I was hungry all the time, but the small amount was better than nothing.

There was no water nor bathroom facilities but they did have a large bucket I could use to relieve myself. A small peephole in the door permitted me to look out into the hallway. The whole situation was calculated to give one a feeling of depression, loneliness, and despair. I found myself worrying about what was going to happen to me, trying to sleep to pass the time, and already devising schemes to escape.

INTERROGATION

My dreams of escape were interrupted when a guard came into my solitary cell and took me through several hallways to an attractively furnished office.

I judged the time to be a little before noon but I had no idea what day of the week. The guard ordered me to sit in a chair in front of a large desk. I sat there for several minutes before a pleasant, youthful-appearing German officer came in. When he entered, the guard who had escorted me from my cell to the office snapped to rigid attention, clicking his heels together sharply, and giving the *Heil Hitler!* salute.

The officer dismissed the guard. I remained seated; I fully expected the officer to order me to my feet but he didn't. He introduced himself, making no effort to shake hands, and sat down at the desk.

He spoke perfect English and seemed eager to be friendly. We carried on a light conversation for several minutes. He mentioned that he had spent several years in the United States; in fact, he had gone to college in the States.

"I returned home to the Fatherland for a visit in 1939," he told me. "I was not permitted to return to the United States." He sounded sincerely regretful.

Later, long after I was home, I learned that during the war the Germans watched for men like him—men with a British or American education and language ability—and trained them in the techniques of skillful interrogation. German intelligence gathering was much more efficient than the Allies realized.

After a while the officer asked me if I cared for a cigarette. Since it had been several days since I'd had anything to smoke, I jumped at the chance. It was a menthol type and smaller than American brands but it really did taste good to me.

After a few minutes of trying to put me at ease, he began to ask me questions. The Army Air Force had informed us of our rights under the Geneva Convention of July 27, 1929 in case we were captured. To all of his questions I responded that I was permitted only to give my name, rank, and serial number.

Many of his questions were regarding my outfit. After I refused to answer each of his questions, he surprised me by supplying the correct answer himself. I guess this was supposed to make me believe the Germans already knew everything and there was no harm in anything I might tell him. This went back and forth for several minutes.

Suddenly the air raid sirens sounded. We heard the distant sound of anti-aircraft fire.

People were running around in the hall outside his office as everyone rushed for the protection of bomb shelters. I was ready to run for shelter too, but again the officer surprised me. "Would you like to remain here in the office and watch the air raid with me?" he asked, as pleasantly as he might have offered me a beer.

I said, "Yes sir, I would."

We went over to the shuttered windows and he parted the slats so we could see out. We must have presented a strange tableau, German officer and captured American airman, as we stood side by side and watched my bombers clobber his city. I guessed the target was the railroad yards as our planes were not directly overhead.

We could see the large formation of American B-17 bombers and the bursts of flack as German anti-aircraft shells exploded in the air around the planes. We could see the vapor trails and the sun's glint on the wings of small German fighter planes as they rose to attack the bombers.

It was a very disturbing sight. My memories of combat were fresh. I could visualize the crews up there. I knew what they were going through. I realized many of them would not be returning to base that day. Some of them might even be POWs with me before long.

I have to admit that it was also a very exciting experience. Considering the position I found myself in, it was high drama indeed and I will never forget the sight. I am glad the German officer decided to view the raid and allowed me to watch with him.

After the all-clear signal sounded we returned to our verbal sparring. The officer asked me a few more questions and then called the guard to take me back to my cell.

I remained there at *Dulag Luft* for a few more days before I was removed once again from my solitary cell and advised that I would be going by train to my permanent *Stalag Luft* camp.

As I was being taken out, I caught a glimpse of an Air Force officer in the hall. I couldn't see his birds, but I felt certain it was Colonel Alkire of the 449th. Had he been shot down after me? Or on a later raid? Even though I passed within a few yards of him, I didn't dare look straight at him or give any sign of recognition. I didn't want to give our German captors any information.

A truck drove me and about twenty other POWs to the Frankfurt train depot, probably the same one that had been bombed a few days before. We could see several damaged trains, rails, and sidings. Our guards placed us aboard a passenger train and we began our trip to what would be our new home.

I believe we must have passed through several large railroad yards and cities on our journey. I remember seeing so much destruction. Several times our cars were shunted off on spur tracks while air raids were going on in the towns. Once again our luck held. Our train was never strafed or bombed and we continued on our way.

LILI MARLENE

We made one stop I recall very vividly because of the song we heard.

Our guards unloaded us at the station in some large town and took us down a flight of steps into a real big underground canteen or maybe it was a bomb shelter. I sensed a somber mood. The place was filled with German military personnel. Everyone I'd seen in Germany—men, women, children, older folks—all seemed to be in some kind of colorful uniform. We prisoners were given bowls of soup and seated around a large table.

While we were eating, the song, "Lili Marlene," was being played over the loud-speaker system. I suppose it was the situation or the atmosphere or something, but I will never forget that moment and the feeling I had as I heard that song. My spirits soared as I listened to the haunting melody. I could almost forget I was a prisoner. I felt as though I could march over a waterfall to the beat of that music.

Long after the war ended and I was finally home again, I could never hear the song without remembering that first time. Eventually I learned something about the history of the words.

41

Hans Leip, a twenty-one-year old German fusilier, wrote the poem during the first World War. The words were set to music in the late 1930s, about the time it was obvious Germany once again was about to go to war. Several singers recorded it but the version sung by Lale Andersen was always the most popular in the Fatherland.

The song became a link between German soldiers, wherever they were, and their families back home. Minister of Propaganda Joseph Goebbels decided the song was too mushy and sentimental and that soldiers needed something more brisk and military sounding. He officially banned the song but no one paid any attention to him.

The unusual thing was "Lili Marlene" became one of the most popular war songs not only with German soldiers but with British and American troops as well. Back in the States the German-born actress Marlene Dietrich and several other singers recorded it in translation:

Underneath the lantern
by the barracks gate
Darling I remember
the way you used to wait.

Vor der Kaserne,
Vor dem grossen Tor
Stand eine Laterne
Und steht sie noch davor.
Wenn wir uns einmal wiedersehn,
Bei der Laterne woll'n wir stehn
Wie einst, Lili Marlene!

STALAG LUFT VI

We stayed at the canteen for a while, grateful for our meager meal and the soothing music. After a while we were ordered aboard the train again and sent on our way.

I am not sure what day it was when we left Frankfurt, but we arrived at our new camp at Heydekrug, East Prussia on February 18, 1944. In the early days of the war most POWs were British and American airmen. At first they were given relatively humane treatment but later in the war Germany's attitude toward POWs changed. POW camps were located in the far eastern part of Germany or its occupied territory to make escape as difficult as possible.

The camp was known as *Stalag Luft* VI and it was located about six kilometers (not quite four miles) from the border of Lithuania and about the same distance from the Baltic Sea. I think the closest town to Heydekrug was a town called Tilsit, forty kilometers (about twenty-five miles) southeast of Heydekrug.

We arrived in the dead of winter. The wind off the Baltic was cold and damp and seemed to cut right through our American uniforms. One of the first things our German captors had done was to shave our heads. From the standpoint of sanitation I guess it was a good thing—head lice were less of a problem if you had no hair—but we scrounged any caps or scarves we could to keep our bald heads warm.

Stalag Luft VI was composed of three large compounds or *Lagers*, with each compound having eight to ten stone and brick barracks and two or more smaller wooden barracks. A cook shack and a storage room for camp supplies were located at one end of each compound which also had a building for showering and washing, although neither had any hot water.

Our quarters had two-man bunks with some tables, stools, and wall shelves.

There were usually sixteen to twenty men to a room. The bunks all had five slats that were supposed to be one-by-six boards, though many of them were much more narrow. We placed our straw mattresses across the slats and altogether it was about as comfortable as lying

(Photo courtesy Greg Hatton)

With nothing much to do, Kriegies sat or stood around. Boredom was as constant as hunger.

on an old-fashioned corrugated washboard. Board shelves along the walls were barely wide enough for us to keep what few articles of clothing or personal toilet items we managed to keep or acquire.

Most of the rooms had two large windows which were tightly shuttered at night. A pot-bellied coal-burning stove stood in the center of the room. We never had enough fuel to keep us comfortably warm.

Each of the barracks had a latrine at the end of a long hall. The "honey-wagon brigade" composed of Russian and Polish POWs came by every few days and emptied the latrines.

Each compound was made secure by an eight-foot high double barbed-wire fence with a four-foot rolled barbed-wire entanglement between the two fences. The compound was laid out in a rectangular shape. Large guard towers stood at each corner of the double-barbed wire fence. Each tower had a mounted machine gun as well as large search lights. One or two guards manned the towers twenty-four hours a day. Guards walked their posts between the towers. At night there were guards we called "ferrets" with trained guard dogs making random walks inside the compound itself.

A rail about twenty-five feet away from the double fence consisted of pieces of one-by-four lumber nailed to the tops of small posts about two feet high. No one was permitted to cross the rail for any purpose or to get any closer to the double fence.

The order concerning the guard- or safety-rail was strictly enforced. We were all made tragically aware of it.

One day a POW was playing ball with several other prisoners and the ball happened to roll under the guardrail toward the security fence. Without thinking what he was doing the ball player jumped over the rail and ran toward the double wire fence to retrieve the ball. We never knew if the guard in the tower saw the ball or not but it made no difference. The guard fired his rifle and killed the POW. None of us was likely to forget the rule after seeing our fellow prisoner shot down.

(Sketch by author)

German guards, armed with machine guns, watched the POW compounds day and night.

NEVER ENOUGH

Food was probably uppermost in our minds. We were always hungry.

The Geneva Convention required that POWs be fed at least as well as the captor nation's soldiers but in practice it didn't work that way. We were given a thin stew or soup of kohlrabi, some barley, and some potatoes. There was a little salt but no other seasonings.

As a general rule we received Red Cross food packets about once a week to supplement our rations. They contained cheese, Spam, corned beef, chocolate D-Bars, and margarine. They also contained canned paté, which wasn't as elegant as it might sound. These packages, meant for one person, were usually shared among as many as four of us.

We prepared our food in the camp's cook shack as it would have been difficult to do much cooking in our barracks. The Germans gave us a few briquettes to heat our quarters. We used them sparingly but occasionally we fixed treats for ourselves—such as toast or sandwiches—on top of our heating stove. Toasting the heavy, soggy black bread made it a little more palatable but not much.

Food was such a treat we tried to eat as slowly as we could to make the meal last as long possible. One guy could outdo us all and that was Jake Routon—but that didn't become a big problem until later.

Our camp leader, or "Man of Confidence," called meetings and passed instructions from the camp commandant down to barracks leaders who passed them on to us.

Technical Sergeant Frank Paules, a minister's son from Lansdale, Pennsylvania was our MOC. I never met him or had a chance to talk to him, but I recognized him when I saw him in the compound. He was a tall, good-looking man and had the respect of all the POWS and even the Germans. I later learned that after the war Paules attended the war crimes trials at Nuremberg and tried to have several cases of prisoner abuse presented—especially the "Run Up the Road" to *Stalag Luft IV* on July 18, 1944.

At irregular intervals—to avoid detection—a "reader" or reporter visited our barracks to pass on news gleaned from a small concealed radio some of the men had managed to put together. The Germans knew or certainly suspected we had a hidden radio somewhere in camp. They made frequent and thorough searches at any time of the day or night hoping to find it. The guards came into our rooms yelling, "*Raus! Raus!*" We had to stand outside until they finished tearing through everything.

For the most part Allied airmen were not assigned to work details—certainly not outside the camp. Germans called us *Terror Flieger* and believed we had special training in terrorism and sabotage. They kept a close watch on us.

The men made some attempts at organized sports and recreation but most of the time we gathered in small groups and entertained ourselves. A few of the men exercised as often as they could by walking the perimeter of the compound. Most of the British POWs had been in camp since their country's entry into the war in September 1939. I used to see some of them walking alone, smiling, waving their arms, and carrying on animated, solitary conversations with themselves.

With so many of us confined to such cramped quarters, conflicts were bound to flare up occasionally but I saw few real fights—mostly just name-calling and insults.

We gave everyone nicknames, especially the guards. We named some for the Seven Dwarfs. One guard was over-size and under-smart—we named him "Big Stoop." I knew who he was when I saw him—you couldn't miss him, he was big as a hangar—but fortunately I never had a run-in with him. His casual cruelty earned him our hatred. After the war when I heard that someone had settled the final score with Big Stoop I was neither surprised nor sorry.

Staff Sergeant Ed Jurist dubbed me "Big Moe" because he said I reminded him of the battleship USS *Missouri*. I wasn't that large but maybe he thought I was that much of a scrapper. Anyway, I chose to take it as a compliment.

We played all the card games we could think of: bridge, canasta, gin rummy, and poker, using cigarettes for money. Sometimes we played checkers, chess, dominos, and even marbles. Many of the POWs borrowed books from the camp's small library and spent their time reading or studying. The guys would do anything to escape the deadly boredom—some even learned to knit with the needles and yarn available to them through the Red Cross.

My favorite pastime was chess and my favorite partner was Ed Jurist. Jurist was a New Yorker who had been an advertising agent for Paramount Studios before the war. He was well educated and outgoing. He was several years my senior and figured—city slicker that he was—he should be able to beat a country bumpkin like me at chess with no trouble. I whipped him nearly every time we played and it made him so mad he could hardly talk.

Now after having described the place where I found myself, as well as some of the conditions under which I would have to live, I must go back to tell about my arrival at *Stalag Luft* VI.

After we were unloaded at the train station, we were transported by truck to the camp. Much to my surprise, one of the first persons I encountered was Chuck LaMarca.

Charles A. ("Chuck") LaMarca

Chuck was one of my crew members but he'd been flying extra as photographer on another plane, the "White Fang." He had been shot down January 14, two weeks before my fateful day. We all presumed that he was dead.

"I never expected to see you again," I told him as we shook hands and then threw our arms around one another.

LaMarca told me he and one of the regular crewmen of the "White Fang" were the only survivors of this ill-fated ship.

I was lucky enough to be assigned to the same barracks with Chuck. We had a great deal to talk about. As soon as we exchanged our stories about how we came to be POWs, we began to talk about how we would escape.

Our Air Force officers had told us if we were taken prisoners and had an opportunity to escape with a fair chance of success, then we should try. We also were encouraged to keep as many enemy troops as possible tied up trying to guard us. I believed it was my duty to attempt to escape if at all possible.

I don't remember how we got together with two other guys who were eager to join in our effort, but they were Jake Routon and Tom Stapleton. Routon was blond, not very tall but well built and muscular. Stapleton had dark hair. He was small with a slight build.

The four of us made an unlikely combination, me a country boy from Texas, LaMarca from Ohio, Routon from Washington state and Tom Stapleton from Rochester, New York. Physically we were all still in good health. None of us had suffered any significant injury when we were shot down. I felt sure that they all had the necessary determination and coolness under pressure to make our attempt to escape a fair possibility.

All things considered, I think we shared a great deal of confidence in each other and in our chances for a successful escape.

Knowing I had buddies who thought the same way I did felt great. The four of us began to pool our information. We checked out every possibility we could think of. We watched how camp security was maintained, how the guards changed shifts, and anything else we thought we could use in furthering our efforts.

The one thing that troubled us most was the random patrol of the ferrets with their dogs. We could think of no way that would guarantee us an edge in avoiding the patrols other than sheer good luck. The ferrets started their patrol as soon as the compound lights came on at dark and continued them until daylight. We knew that for a fact—we stayed up at night and peeped through the shuttered windows to check them out. We listened to the guards walking by the buildings and talking to their dogs.

We knew that once we got outside the compound there was no concealment for about a half-mile, but at least there were no searchlights or dogs to contend with on the outside. Getting through that double wire fence and past the guards and dogs wouldn't be easy but we were determined to try.

We knew that, so far, no one had escaped successfully from *Stalag Luft* VI but this only strengthened our determination. Even a failed attempt at escape made life rougher for every POW in camp. For this reason most camps had a Security Man who reviewed escape plans, evaluated the odds, and supplied such things as wirecutters and maps and compasses.

One of our barracks leaders called our attention to a British POW named Patty Kerr. I don't know why Kerr was in a position to give us assistance but he may have been a Security Man. We sought him out and told him of our determination to escape.

"Let me know as soon as you've made your plans and tell me what you need," Kerr said. "I'll help you all I can."

We debated for some time before we decided we would try to cut through the double barbed-wire fence. We had discovered a certain location in the *Lager* where a shallow drainage ditch ran through the compound and through the fence. The ditch started very close to one of the smaller wooden barracks built on piers about one foot high on the low side and probably two feet high at the location closest to the shallow ditch. We figured the ditch, being about a foot deep near the guardrail, would offer us some cover up to that point.

The ditch shallowed out almost completely from the guardrail to the fence which was still a good twenty-five feet away. However, once you got within about four feet of the fence, the ditch deepened to about three feet and ran right beside one of the floodlight poles, through the fence and underneath a little foot bridge over which the guards crossed as they walked their post a few feet from the outside fence.

We paid careful attention to the timing of the guards as they walked their posts on the outside perimeter. We knew when they changed and how long it took them to go from one end of the fence to the other. We took into consideration the time the moon came up and how much snow was on the ground. Armed with as much information as we felt useful, we were ready to go back to Patty Kerr.

Patty and the four of us went over our plans in great detail and it was Patty's opinion that we had a reasonable chance of making our escape if we had good luck. At least he felt that it was worth giving us the necessary items we needed to make the effort.

Our own government-issued escape kits had been found and confiscated when we were first captured, so we had nothing we could use. Patty was able to supply us with a wirecutter, a small compass, sticks to prop the wire entanglement up, and a small hand-drawn map. We never inquired as to how he was able to make these things available and he never volunteered any information. We knew it was best that we have no knowledge of his activities and let it go at that.

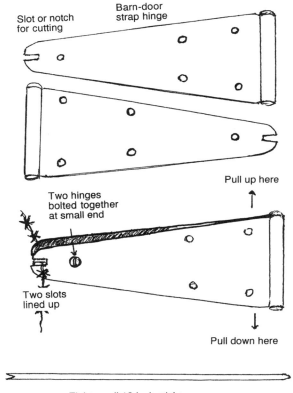

Slot or notch for cutting

Barn-door strap hinge

Two hinges bolted together at small end

Two slots lined up

Pull up here

Pull down here

Eight small 18-inch sticks to prop up the barbed wire

(Sketch by author)

Figure 1

The simple wirecutter had been made from a large barn-door type hinge. The pin had been removed from where the hinge folds and then the two small pointed ends were bolted together. With the hinges bolted together and positioned side by side, a slot had been cut across one edge near the bolted end. You placed the slot over a piece of wire, pulled the large end of the hinges apart and cut the wire. The cutters were crude but effective. As a blacksmith's son I had to admire the inventor's ingenuity.

The tiny compass Patty gave me was about a quarter-inch thick and about half an inch in diameter. You could easily hide it in your mouth or in your pants fly under the last button. The hand-made map gave us the general directions we would need if we were to make our way to the free city of Danzig in northern Poland. We didn't realize that the "free city" had been taken over by the Germans in September 1939. We thought if we could reach that port we might be able to catch a ship back to freedom.

We tucked away all the items we had received as well as about six or eight eighteen-inch long sticks which we intended to use to prop up the barbed-wire fence entanglement. We told our plans to our fellow prisoners and they agreed to conceal our disappearance as long as they could.

At last we were ready to make our attempt. I would be less than truthful to say that we weren't uptight about the attempt—my stomach knotted every time I remembered the POW who'd been shot dead just for chasing a ball—but there was no way that any of us would back out. We made a fair effort to limit the number of people who knew of our plan, but even then I suppose our whole barracks was aware of it by the time we were ready to execute it. Many of them would be involved in helping to supply a few extra pieces of clothing or food and in trying to cover for us at roll call.

I'd been in *Stalag Luft* VI less than a full month but I'd been set on escape since the moment of my capture. During the day of March 11, 1944 everything felt right to us. We decided we would execute our plan that night.

We hastily prepared the small pack of food we had managed to swap or beg from the others. This consisted mostly of a few chocolate D-Bars, a small amount of bread, some ersatz jam, and a couple of packs of cigarettes.

ESCAPE NUMBER ONE

The time was right—we just knew it. Excited and fearful at the same time, we hastily dressed ourselves in several layers of clothing. We'd need to keep warm but we couldn't risk handicapping ourselves trying to carry many bundles so we wore everything we could.

All the prisoners would be locked in their barracks for the night at curfew, so right before that a number of our fellow POWs gathered near our escape site— talking, smoking, acting natural—and screened us from view.

We crawled underneath the small wooden barracks next to the drainage ditch.

Once we were under the barracks we crawled to the deepest, blackest point. The guards would never be able to see us there unless they got down on their hands and knees and deliberately searched for us. I hoped they'd have no reason to do so.

We crouched in the darkness, scarcely daring to breathe. My heart was beating so loudly I was afraid the sound would give us away. After a few minutes passed we heard the bugle blow for curfew and we listened as the guards locked up all the barracks. Too late for us to sneak back in now even if we had been willing to admit defeat so soon. We had at that moment cast our fate to the God of Good Fortune.

We remained hidden under the barracks for two long hours while we waited for the cover of night. As soon as it began to get dark, the guards turned on the area floodlights that lit up every corner of the compound. The search lights on the guard towers began to crisscross the compound. We could see the guards walking their posts on the outside of the double barbed-wire fence. We knew that very soon other guards with their German shepherd dogs would begin making random walks around the compound.

I am sure that each of us must have had secret thoughts of giving in to our fears and trying to get back to our cozy barracks—bad as prison camp life was, it was reasonably safe if you stuck to the rules. But our pride and our determination to escape prevailed.

Finally we felt the proper time had come to move out. We began to make our way out from under the secure darkness of our hiding place and to move toward the drainage ditch. We were slithering along on our bellies, flattened as closely to the ground as possible. Each time the search light swept toward us we froze, hoping that the dark earth between the numerous patches of snow and the small shadows cast by the uneven terrain would help us to blend with the ground.

I was in the lead. When I reached the deeper part of the ditch before it shallowed out near the guard rail, I stopped and waited for the other three to join me.

Our plan was simple: I would take the wirecutter

and the sticks and crawl over to the fence while the guard was at the far end of his rounds and facing away from where I would be cutting the fence. My three buddies would keep watch. If they signaled me I would know they figured the returning guard was getting too close. I would join them where they were lying in the ditch.

After a moment I nodded that I was going to make my way to the fence. I started snaking myself underneath the forbidden guardrail and toward the compound fence. From the guardrail all the way to within a few feet of the fence I found little cover. The ditch became even more shallow. There were some concealing shadows and visual distortions from the melted snow and uneven terrain. I tried to take advantage of them, creeping from darkness to darkness. I stopped, held my breath, flattened myself and tried to look like a clod of dirt each time the searchlights swept over me. I expected to be discovered any moment and to feel machine gun bullets ripping into my body. When the light passed I crept slowly along until I finally reached the fence.

(Photo courtesy Greg Hatton)

This photograph of the POW compound shows the forbidden strip, the double barbed-wire fences, and the guard tower.

I knew even before I reached it that I would not risk crossing back from the fence to where my buddies were waiting. I began to use my wirecutter. I tried to be very cautious but in the chill night air each cut I made exploded in my ears like an artillery shell. They must be able to hear my noise clear to *Wehrmacht* headquarters in Berlin!

After I cut four or five wires, I heard my companions' hissed signal indicating the guard was approaching and that I should return to their location. I signaled with my flattened palm that I was going to remain there by the fence. I can't imagine the

(Sketch by author)

Night of March 11, 1944. Gann cut a hole through the barbed-wire fence while the guard made his rounds in the opposite direction. His three budies waited anxiously for his signal.

consternation and disbelief that must have flashed through their minds when I departed from our carefully laid plans. I hunkered down and remained as motionless as a rabbit. Even though I was hiding less than eight feet from the guard's path, I gambled that by remaining at the fence I had a better chance of dodging detection.

Don't let him see me, I prayed. *Don't let him look down*! I was directly beneath the floodlight and sticking as closely as possible to the light-pole.

The light was focused to illuminate the center of the compound, thus offering me some shadow underneath. The ditch became deeper as it went through the fence and I took advantage of this by keeping even closer to the fence. I think the best thing I had going for me was that the guard's eyes were trained out into the compound. He didn't expect to find someone almost under his feet.

(Sketch by author)

I was scared to death. I held my breath so long that even after the guard had passed by I had to force myself to exhale.

As soon as the guard was far enough away, I started to cut wires. Each time the guard approached, I pressed myself against the fence. The guard passed by. I cut more wire. I'm sure my buddies were as frightened as I was and felt helpless besides. All they could do was crouch, wait, and pray.

I broke through the wires of the inside fence. After the guard passed by again I used several of my sticks to prop up the mesh and entanglement wire. I heard the urgent hiss of my companion. I'd been so busy I'd almost forgotten to watch for the guard. I began to back out of the hole I had cut through the wire. Some of the barbs snagged my bulky clothing. I was trapped, unable to pull loose. Try as hard as I might, it was impossible for me to get loose without going forward. By then the guard was almost on top of me. I dared not make a sound or movement or I would surely be detected and shot.

I had no alternative. I had to lie there and wait for my certain death. I had visions of being shot right there inside the barbed-wire fence. What on Earth made me so cocksure I could escape when others had failed? What would happen to my companions who had trusted my judgment and depended on me?

Once again the shadows, my dark clothing, the guard's failure to look down, and most of all, the Good Lord's help spared me.

As soon as the guard passed, I inched my way forward in my wire trap and managed to extract myself. Even as cold as the night was, I was sweating inside my bulky clothing. I made several more cuts, stopping and backing out of the opening I was making each time the guard passed. I was almost ready to start cutting on the outside fence when I heard the hiss of my companions at the same time I heard the sound of an approaching bicycle.

I had no time to do anything but to lie flat, my cheek pressed to the frozen ground, and watch a camp guard on a bicycle coming along the path. A large German police dog trotted along in front of him. I realized this was really the end. The guard might not be paying enough attention to notice me but a scattering of shadows wouldn't be enough to prevent a trained dog from catching the body-scent of my fear.

I will never understand the hand of Fate. The guard and his dog passed right by me and moved off along the path. Once again I was saved. I was so weak with relief it was a moment or two before I could roll over and go back to work.

I made the final cuts in the wire of the outside fence. The guard was now at the farthest end of his post and walking away from me. I squirmed through the fence and onto the guard path. I crawled a few feet to the foot bridge and hid underneath it.

I was now out of the compound enclosed by the double fence, the watch towers and guards, but I wasn't in the clear yet. Halfway to freedom is not enough. I looked around to find myself in a compound still under construction. A single fence surrounded its perimeter.

I huddled under the footbridge for half an hour or more while the German guard tromped back and forth across the bridge what seemed like a hundred times. I lay there, scarcely breathing, trying to get some idea of his pattern or frequency. It was our good fortune that the small amount of water beneath the footbridge was shallow and frozen over. If I'd been crouched in water I'd have frozen too.

The cold winter moon had come up and made the night as bright as day. I finally decided to make my way toward the fence that encircled the incomplete compound. I crawled almost to the fence and into a foundation trench. Then I waited for my companions to follow me.

And waited.

They were not going to come through the fence and I was going to be left alone. They hadn't been caught—I would have heard the commotion if the guards had found them. Maybe they had changed their minds. Maybe they had waited so long for me to cut through that they'd given up. Maybe even now as I waited they were trying to sneak back into the barracks. I can't honestly say I blamed them.

But what about me? I'd come too far to risk going back—I'd be shot for sure if I tried that. I decided to give up on the other three and try to make it on my own.

I was about to make my way to the other fence when I noticed a dark shadowy something moving about halfway between me and the footbridge. I blinked my eyes and strained to make it out. Then I saw two more dark shapeless lumps creeping toward me. My hopes soared.

OUTSIDE AND ON
THE RUN

In a few minutes I was joined by LaMarca, Routon, and Stapleton.

We shook hands, slapped each other on the back and quietly congratulated ourselves on making it this far. We might have been tempted to take a minute or two to rest and catch our breath but our adrenaline level was too high. We had to keep going.

We bellied our way to the last fence and looked the situation over. Since there were no guards or floodlights around the unfinished new compound, I was able to make short work of cutting my way through the fence.

We were finally free of *Stalag Luft* VI.

We each knew this was only the first step. Real freedom was still only a remote possibility. Even though we were at last free from the camp, the guards, the dogs, and the tower searchlights, we had sense enough to know we had to crawl on our bellies for several hundred yards before we dared get up on our hands and knees.

We crawled for probably half a mile before we stood up and stretched muscles knotted by nerves and exertion. Using our tiny compass, we headed in the direction of the Lithuanian border. After we had walked for about a mile in the moonlight we passed a rather large pond. I threw my nifty little wirecutters out into the middle of the water, heard them *plop!* and watched the widening ripples. Rather too optimistically I figured I'd never need wirecutters again.

We continued to walk until almost daylight. We were satisfied that we were now well within the borders of Lithuania. The countryside was fairly well forested. We came to what looked like a replanted forest of young trees, all in straight rows about four feet apart. We decided to stop there and try to get some sleep until nightfall when it was safe to move on.

We ate a small portion of our bread and some jam and then attempted to make ourselves comfortable there in the foot-deep snow. We were cold and miserable. We tried "sandwiching"—each taking turns being the one to lie in the middle for body-warmth—but most of the time we sat huddled together waiting for nightfall.

When night fell we'd been free almost twenty-four hours. We started moving in what we hoped was the general direction of the Memel River. I found myself wishing I'd paid more attention to all those pink and green and yellow and lavender blobs in my geography textbook back home in Del Valle but it wouldn't have mattered. Years of war had changed all boundaries.

We hoped to follow the Memel River which we falsely believed would lead us toward Danzig. We walked most of the second night out of camp, trying to avoid being seen by anyone. The farther we got away from camp the safer we'd feel. We were afraid the whole German army was out beating the bushes looking for us.

One thing we learned in a hurry was to watch for geese. They could detect us a mile away, even at night.

Every little farm seemed to have a gaggle of geese guards. It was almost impossible to avoid being discovered by them. As soon as they knew we were near they started honking loud enough to wake the dead. I suppose the honking geese may have helped us. They kept us alert and we exercised a little more caution as we either approached or skirted around the house or barn where they were penned.

After about seventy-two hours of walking at night and trying to hide and sleep in the day, we felt safe enough to change our routine and walk in daylight. We were careful to stick to the edge of the woods and keep out of sight as much as possible. We made better time traveling this way. We approached some of the farm houses along the way, cautiously at first and then with growing boldness. We asked for food. Although none of us knew German, we had learned the words for eat (*essen*), bread (*brot*), and we used sign language as well.

As long as we were not in Germany all we had to do was say "American" and "flyer" and most of the people would be all smiles. They were very friendly after they learned who we were. They shared whatever they had with us—mostly coarse black bread and uncooked salt pork or sow belly.

Even as hungry as we were, this sort of fare was not long in giving us what country folks called the "backdoor trots." We spent our time hastily pulling down several layers of clothing and pulling them back up.

Farm families often permitted us to sleep in their barns or haylofts. In that part of the country barns seemed to be built connected to the houses. None of the places we stayed had any means of communication— no telephones or two-way radios—so we felt fairly safe no one would summon the nearest Nazis to come and get us. Nevertheless we kept a close lookout to be sure no one left the house once we were bedded down.

On the night of March 17, 1944 after having walked all day and late into the night, we came to a rather large house located very near the town of Jabarkous, Lithuania.

As usual, our approach was heralded by honking geese. When we saw a coal oil lamp glowing inside, we decided to ask for food and a place to sleep. We knocked on the door and a very friendly man welcomed us. To our surprise he spoke fairly good English.

As soon as he learned we were Americans, he called the rest of his family in to meet us. His wife and two daughters, about twelve- and thirteen-year-olds, came out of the back rooms to see what we Americans looked like. I will never forget how big-eyed they were at seeing what I suppose were their first Americans. They were the most friendly folks you would ever want to meet. Since the man could speak English, we carried on a conversation for most of the night.

He told us he had been some kind of city employee or minor official in the town of Jabarkous. Then the Germans took over. Everything had changed—and not for the better. Clearly he had no use for Germans and not much more for Russians.

He was fond of the Americans. He said he could hardly wait for us to win the war—he was certain we would do so. His wife fixed us the first good meal we'd had in a long while. Then our friendly host gave us a place to sleep in the house. This was a welcome change from drafty barns or snow-covered woods.

Early the next morning we ate a hearty breakfast and made ready to continue our journey. Before leaving I asked the man if he would trade a pair of his trousers for a pair of my army pants. He agreed. He brought out a pair of black trousers. I pulled them on over my other trousers and we were ready to leave. I still don't have any idea why I wanted to trade for the trousers, but I was very proud of them at the time. I will never forget the hospitality of that good family.

During our conversation with the man, we learned that Jabarkous lay alongside the Memel River. The town was divided by a rather large creek that flowed into the Memel. A bridge crossed the creek.

"You must go right down the main street of the town to get to the bridge. The creek is very deep and very cold," he warned us.

We understood that we would have to use the bridge if we hoped to cross the creek. Armed with this valuable information, with food in our bellies, and with considerably improved morale we set out for Jabarkous.

Before we got to the edge of the town, we stopped in a large gully near the bank of the river and smoked a cigarette. We finished our smoke and started into the town. We'd been avoiding people but now we were planning to walk down the main street. We observed that we were taller than the Lithuanian civilians and we were dressed differently.

"We'd better split up," I decided, "so we won't attract too much attention. Tom and I'll walk about three hundred feet ahead of you all and on the other side of the street."

To our relief the very few people who were on the street paid little attention to us. We walked all the way through town without any problems. All was going well—in fact, far easier than I had expected. We almost had it made. I began to get a cocky swagger in my step.

I turned to signal LaMarca and Routon to cross the street and join us, when I noticed a man and woman coming from town in a horse-drawn wagon. They were riding on a spring-board seat and the wagon had sideboards about two feet high.

I watched them, thinking how strange it was that while everyone else was slowly meandering along, the couple in the wagon seemed to be in such a big hurry.

As the wagon drew near LaMarca and Routon, the man reined the team to an abrupt halt. Four uniformed police jumped up from the floorboards of the wagon, aimed their rifles at the four of us and yelled for us to halt.

We had no choice. We raised our hands into the air and waited for the police to climb from the wagon and search us. We were bitterly discouraged. Just when it seemed things were really going our way!

We quickly identified ourselves as American flyers. To my surprise our captors seemed reluctant to take us back to the police station once they knew who we were.

We learned later that a good citizen of the town had spotted us while we were taking a break and smoking a cigarette on the bank of the Memel. He mistook us for Russians and rushed into town to inform the lone German soldier stationed there. The soldier ordered the local police to go pick us up.

The police had no choice but take us to the station. They placed us in their small one-room jail. This all happened about noon on March 18—only seven days after our escape from *Stalag Luft* VI.

Word must have spread quickly about the Americans being held in jail. In no time a great number of the Jabarkous population crowded in to see us and talk to us. The first question the townspeople asked was, "Are you Catholics?"

Only LaMarca was Roman Catholic but the rest of us didn't want to disappoint our new friends. We assured them we were all Catholics and that pleased them. They brought all kinds of soup and bread and other good things to eat. They were so friendly and so sorry to see us in jail that we were certain they would find some way to release us. In the meantime we were getting full, fat, and happy.

I still believe the police would have liked nothing better than to let us go free but I am sure they were afraid of the consequences. The German soldier who sent them after us was standing right there watching every move. And the chief of police, who seemed to be some sort of German sympathizer, was pretty proud of catching four unarmed American escapees.

We remained in the jail overnight, though it would have been easy enough for us to break out of the flimsy and rundown jail. We thought about it but the chance of quick recapture was too high.

The next morning the police chief and a couple of his men came with a large horse-drawn buggy to take us into the German town of Tilsit. We were handcuffed and loaded into the buggy with a driver. The police chief and one officer followed us on horseback. The townspeople all came to wave goodby as we rode out of town.

As we traveled through the dense woods toward Tilsit we expected the townspeople to swoop down on our buggy like a scene from a Western movie, take us away from the police, and set us free. Much to our sorrow that did not happen. Probably they'd never seen a Western movie and the thought never occurred to them.

FORT KÖNIGSLOUISE

Our visions of a dramatic rescue faded. We arrived in Tilsit and the Jabarkous police took us to the German army post and released us into German custody.

The only good thing that happened, as far as we were concerned, was watching the humiliation the Jabarkous chief suffered as he saluted the German desk sergeant about four times before the sergeant acknowledged his presence. We could tell the German was deliberately ignoring the chief and we got a little satisfaction out of that.

The Germans placed us in the Tilsit jail and there we remained until March 28. We soon learned that the food given to prisoners in the civilian jails of Germany was in short supply. We began to remember the food in our *Stalag*—it had been a feast compared to what we received while we were held in the civilian jails.

Finally we were transferred to a German army prison called Fort Königslouise, near the town of Königsberg, East Prussia.

Fort Königslouise was all underground and well camouflaged, being completely concealed by a growth of timber and brush. As best we could tell, it was used only as a military jail and for the most part held German soldiers charged with infractions such as failing to salute an officer or going AWOL. Obviously it was not a maximum-security prison.

The four of us were taken down a long tunnel-like hallway to a very large room off to one side. The rock walls of the fortress were curved like the inside of a Quonset hut. The room we were placed in was divided down the middle by a wooden wall about six feet high with wire mesh running the rest of the way to the ceiling.

Against the walls on both sides of the divider was a ten-foot long board platform about eight feet wide and two feet high. The platform served as a bed for the prisoners. Wooden doors from both rooms opened into the long hallway.

It was in Fort Königslouise that the three of us— LaMarca, Stapleton, and I—decided to kill Jake Routon.

Jake's habit of eating slowly had been bad enough at *Stalag* VI. In our cramped room it was maddening. Our captors gave us so little to eat the rest of us wolfed our food down. But there Jake Routon would be, daintily munching on a tiny bread crust, crumb by precious crumb. He lived only because we turned our attention away from him to the more important matter of escape.

We hadn't risked our lives and come this far toward freedom only to be returned to a *Stalag*.

As soon as we were placed in the room we found there were at least a dozen or more German soldiers being held in the room on the other side from us. They were all fairly young and seemed friendly enough. We looked over the wire partition and carried on a conversation with one or two of then who could speak a little English.

I will never forget the story one of them told us about his experiences while fighting the Russians on the Eastern front.

He said the Russian civilians had lined up, hand in hand—men, women and children—and charged the German lines. A few might be armed with pitchforks or other farm tools—no other type of weapons. The soldier said the Germans fired their guns and mowed the civilians down like so much fodder in the fields. He guessed the Russians were determined to make the Germans use up their ammunition, even if that's all they could do to defend their homeland.

The soldiers told us several stories about action on the Eastern front. We could see that these Germans were glad to be away from that part of the war.

Even while we were carrying on our friendly conversations with the soldiers, we were making plans to break out of our part of the jail room we were in.

We had been thoroughly searched before we had been locked in the room. So when I found and automatically picked up an empty shell casing I was able to keep it although I had no notion of how I could use it. It appeared to be about a .30.30-caliber. The casing had rolled underneath the edge of the platform bed and I figured that one of the German soldiers had carelessly dropped it and failed to pick it up.

I decided to see if I could make the casing into a key that would fit the lock of our cell. The lock was a square inset type and I shaped the shell in such a way that it would slide down over the square inset. The problem was that the lock could only be reached from

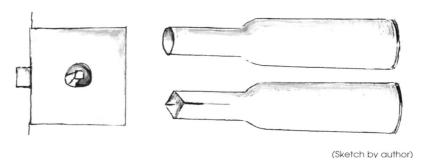

(Sketch by author)

Figure 2

the outside. Using my POW tag, I removed some boards from the wall adjoining the door.

Our guards checked on us so infrequently that none of this would have been a problem if it had not been for the friendly young German soldiers. Curious as baby jaybirds, they were constantly poking their heads over the wire partition to look at us—just as we had done at first with them.

We had to wait until late at night before we could begin prying off a board—the slightest noise might alert the soldiers. After nights of silent work we managed to remove a board which we then placed back in position so as to appear we hadn't tampered with it. While we removed the board, we also kept tabs on the outside guards' schedule as they came around to check on us. Since our cell was pretty well lighted, the guard usually would glance through the peephole in the door, mutter something like, *"Ah, gut, die schlafen,"* and continue on his rounds.

One night shortly after the guard made his round, I eased the already loosened board from the wall, reached through the opening with my key and turned the lock in the door. We carefully replaced the board, stepped outside our cell then re-locked the cell door.

Once again we had made a small step in the direction of freedom.

What if our curious fellow-prisoners peered over the divider and noticed our absence? Would they alert the guards? We started at once to move off down the long tunnel, not knowing at what minute someone might come out of one of the many side rooms or passageways and stop us. The slightest noise seemed to echo loudly. We quietly tiptoed our way until we found a ramp leading up to a landing with a door that opened to the outside.

The door was unlocked. We couldn't believe our good fortune. We stepped into the fresh night air and bright moonlight. We had gone only a hundred feet or so when we found ourselves at the edge of the roof. Lucky we had so much moonlight. Otherwise we'd have stepped right off the fortress and fallen some thirty feet onto the stone courtyard below.

We swung around and didn't stop until our feet were on solid ground. Then we got our bearings and set off once more in the general direction of Danzig. We walked until it began to get light. Then we hid out in some dense brush while we slept and rested for several hours. We'd long since used the meager rations we'd started out with. We hadn't been fed well at Fort Königslouise and we were hungry. But we quenched our thirst with melted snow and forgot our hunger in the excitement of being on the run again.

Later on in the afternoon we decided to take a chance and leave our shelter. We began walking again, trying to stick to the edge of timber and out of sight as much as possible. We walked until sometime after midnight, when we hid out and slept until well into the next morning. This time we didn't dare ask for food or water or help of any kind. We were back on German territory and we knew we would be captured at once.

As we walked we tried to follow a railroad track that seemed to go in the general direction we were headed. We thought of trying to hop a train when it stopped at one of the small stations along the way. We made several attempts to get into position so we could run alongside the train as it left the station but we could never find a hiding place close enough. The trains started so fast and gained speed so quickly we found it impossible to catch them.

At one station we found a good-sized pile of logs stacked alongside the tracks. We sneaked up to the logs and hid behind them in the dark for a long time, listening for the whistle that would announce the train. Finally the train approached. To our disappointment it was a passenger train. We knew better than to try to board it—we'd be recognized for what we were in a heartbeat. We let it pass and gave up on our scheme to ride a train.

We decided to leave our place of concealment and continue on foot.

We passed a small airfield. We crouched out of sight and talked it over. Could we steal a plane? That would be a joke on the Germans if we took one of their own planes right under their noses. We watched a guard patrolling inside the wire-fenced perimeter. Cutting our way out of the *Stalag* had been risky enough. We had no intention of cutting our way into a sure-fire mess—and anyway, I'd thrown the cutters in the lake. We vetoed the scheme.

We walked for over an hour and realized we had to dodge around more than usual trying to avoid being seen. The day was beautiful, almost spring-like, and a great many people were out strolling about. Finally it dawned on us—it must be Easter Sunday. That was the reason for all the activity.

We noticed a rather large growth of timber and underbrush on a hillside not too far from our location. We decided the best thing to do was to head for it and hide out for the rest of the day. We made our way safely to cover and we had gone several hundred feet into the brush when we came upon a slight rise.

We approached the crest of the rise and looked down onto railroad tracks running back into a large tunnel. We dropped down on our stomachs and lay there discussing what to do next. Maybe we should follow the tracks. Maybe we should try again to hop a train—we'd tried that before but the German trains were always too fast for us. By the time you knew one coming it was already past you.

Suddenly I heard the unmistakable *clack!* of a rifle being cocked behind my back.

I cautiously looked back over my shoulder. A German soldier stood behind us. With his rifle he motioned for us to stand up, put our hands in the air, and walk down to the railroad track and the tunnel.

We soon came to understand we unwittingly had walked up onto the submarine torpedo arsenal at Pillau in East Prussia.

At the tunnel the soldiers kept us waiting in an office for about an hour until Gestapo agents came to collect us. There were four of them. They were a very unfriendly bunch and made it clear they'd just as soon shoot us as not. Late in the war all POW affairs came under the *Reichsführer*. The SS and the Gestapo took control of the camps.

They threw us into a large car and headed out with us.

We wound up in a civilian jail in Königsberg. The Gestapo didn't waste much of their time interrogating us. I figured they knew who we were. They knew they hadn't caught any bigtime espionage agents and that we were not planning to blow up the submarine arsenal or anything.

This time our captors separated us and placed each of us in a small cell with seven or eight Russian and Polish prisoners.

These poor souls were nothing but skin and bones. Their eyes were dull and listless and sunken—one can only imagine the horror and suffering they had been through. We never knew for what crime they were being held, but I'm afraid very few of them survived.

THAT CRAZY AMERICAN!

As soon as I was locked in the cell with those poor creatures I began to pace back and forth and yell for the guard to come to the cell door.

I can recall how frightened the other prisoners were—they were certain they had a raving madman for a cellmate but they were even more desperately afraid of their German guards. They cringed against the wall as far away from me as they could get.

When someone responded to my shouts and came to the cell peephole, I insisted that I was an American soldier and a prisoner of war and that the Geneva Convention required that I be placed in a POW camp and given food, clothing, and proper housing.

"You do not look like an American soldier to me," one guard said, looking me over coldly. The guards insisted that I was now a civilian and that I was to stay where I was. They made no further comment.

I looked down at myself. The remnants of my American uniform were ragged and dirty and I was wearing the black trousers I'd swapped from the Lithuanian farmer. I sure wouldn't have passed inspection with the 449th Bombardment Group.

I pitied the poor Russians and Poles but every time I looked at my fellow prisoners—dull-eyed, listless, without the will to go on living—I became more frantic. How long would it take under these demoralizing conditions for me to be the same? I swore I'd rather die trying to escape than to end up like them.

I would look at those pathetic souls and then I'd bang on the door again, scream for the guards, and yell until I was hoarse: "I'm an American soldier! I demand to be treated as a prisoner of war under the Geneva Convention!"

I found out after the war that Russia had never signed the Convention, so neither Russia nor Germany felt obligated to observe the rules with each other. Some 3,000,000 Russians prisoners died from hunger and exposure or were killed in Germany. German POWs fared as badly as the Russians. As many as half the German POWs in Russia were killed or died from harsh conditions.

The cell I found myself in was about six feet by ten feet. There were two buckets, one for water, the other for a slop jar. A very small table was the only furniture. There were no beds of any kind, not even a raised platform. We all had to sleep on the floor. Even then, some of us had to sleep sitting up. The ceiling was probably ten feet high with one small window near the very top.

This window was about twelve inches in size. I discovered I could climb up on the table and look down into the small atrium or courtyard in the center of the building. I soon learned that the courtyard was used as an exercise area for the prisoners. Each day the guards came to the cell and took all of the others out. I was always left there alone and at first I didn't know where the others were going. After the prisoners and guards were gone, I climbed up on the small table, looked down into the courtyard and saw that the guards were having the prisoners exercise.

On one occasion I called the guards and asked to see their sergeant. I was finally taken to an office where an officer was seated behind a small desk. I repeated my story—that I was an American soldier, a prisoner of war, and that the Geneva Convention was not being carried out.

His remark was that I was clearly a civilian and therefore not protected by the terms of the Geneva Convention. I showed him the body lice and bedbugs crawling all over my clothes.

"Hah! Those are your little *paesan*—your friends and countrymen," he said. Maybe he used the word "paesan" to try to impress me that he could speak Italian as well as German and English. He'd have had a hard time in any language trying to convince me that those pests were my friends as they were about to eat me up.

The guards then hustled me back to the cell at gun point and shoved me in with the terrified prisoners. They had probably prayed I wouldn't come back to cause more trouble for everyone.

We had not had a bath during the whole time that we had been away from *Stalag Luft* VI. Our multiple layers of clothing had not been laundered. I soon found myself sitting on the floor in the cell with all the other prisoners—we went over our clothes like monkeys picking fleas. When we took off our layers of clothing and shook them, the dead dry skin from our bodies sifted to the floor like snowflakes.

To make matters even more unbearable, the air in the cell was so foul and humid that I started blowing a thick yellow mucous from my nose almost as soon as I was placed in the cell. I knew if I stayed there much longer I would be in the same pathetic condition as my fellow cellmates.

I had no intention of letting that happen.

I began to plot how I could overpower the guards and escape. I shaped a fragment of the wooden table into a plug that I could insert into the door lock to keep the mechanism from closing properly. Before I could do anything foolish, three guards came and took me out. They marched me down to the office where they had already brought LaMarca, Routon, and Stapleton. We'd been in our separate cells about three weeks.

The guards brandished their weapons and made it clear they meant to shoot us if we so much as made a wrong move. All this time while the sergeant of the guards was shaking his gun at us he was shouting in a loud voice.

LaMarca or one of the others asked me, "What's he saying?"

"It's the same old crap," I told them. "They're going to shoot our butts off if we try to get away."

As soon as I had finished my loose translation, the sergeant ran over to me—right up in my face—and drew back his hand as if he were about to strike me. I felt myself leaning tensely toward him, fully expecting a blow across my face, but for some reason he dropped his hand to his side and only yelled louder.

I have never considered myself as a tush hog or a mean person, but on the other hand I don't ever recall being hit that I didn't strike back. My worst fear—being beaten while not being able to defend myself—seemed about to come true. I knew he wanted an excuse to kill us all. I hoped I could exercise good judgment and take the blow if he hit me.

The sergeant apparently decided he'd put on enough of a show for us and for the guards. The jail guards handcuffed us, escorted us downstairs and turned us over to four waiting SS troopers. They seemed to take some sadistic pleasure in informing us that they were returning us to our prison camp, *Stalag Luft* VI. They loaded us into the back of a canvas-covered truck. The SS troops got in with us and we started for our camp. We were removed from the prison there at Königsberg on the second or third of May. We arrived without incident at our POW camp late that same night.

I suppose the thing I recall most clearly about our return was the manner in which the SS troops treated us. They made it very clear they considered us to be very dangerous men. They let us know they would not hesitate to shoot us if we gave them the slightest provocation. They gave us no opportunity to talk to each other. I am sure they had heard of our two prior escapes. They had no intention of letting us break away again—not on their watch.

As soon as we reached our camp—probably around midnight—we were taken immediately to the camp stockade. After our camp guards thoroughly searched us they placed us in solitary confinement. I drew a small amount of satisfaction that during all the searches to which I had been subjected, none of the guards had ever discovered the small compass I kept hidden below the bottom button in the fly of my pants.

Sometime early the next morning, all four of us were once again brought from our cells, this time to the camp's delousing room. As soon as I learned that we were to be deloused I slipped the hidden compass from my pants fly and placed it in my mouth. I didn't know what might happen to my clothing and I sure didn't want to take a chance on losing it.

We were stripped of all our clothing and placed in a room where we were given soap and allowed a hot shower. This was my first hot water since before I was shot down and the first bath for any of us since before our escape on March 11.

All of us had lost considerable weight while we were away from camp and I do believe we lost several more pounds as a result of scrubbing under the hot shower. We were not nearly as emaciated as the poor Russians and Poles we'd had for company for three weeks, but we made joking remarks to each other about our bony ribs, skinny legs and baggy buttocks. I think I must have lost forty pounds—down from 175 pounds to about 135. I am sure the others had lost equal amounts.

After we finished our shower, the guards returned our clothing to us. The clothes had not been washed but they had been baked in a hot oven to kill the lice and God knows what other creatures had taken up residence in them.

The first thing I did when I got my deloused clothing back was to take my little compass from my mouth and replace it in the fly of my trousers beneath the bottom button. Although I didn't know it at the time, I would use this very small instrument on two more occasions and manage to keep it with me all the way back to liberty and the United States where I finally lost or misplaced it.

As soon as we put our clothes on, we were returned to solitary confinement. We were to remain there—for how long we did not know.

Although solitary confinement was rough here in the regular camp, it was nothing compared to the time we had spent at Königsberg. The only good part was that we knew we were back under the Geneva Convention. The cells we occupied were small, but at least they had bunks with straw mattresses and the ventilation was good.

We were constantly hungry. For breakfast we were fed only a thin slice of black bread with a little of some sort of jam smeared on it. Then at night we got a small bowl of kohlrabi soup. The food had no flavor, no pleasant aroma, and precious little nutrition. Once a week we received a pretty good meal usually consisting of stew and a few small baked potatoes. I remember I thought those were the best potatoes I had ever eaten.

Our guards at the camp stockade were fairly friendly. One in particular, known as Fritz, spoke a little English. Fritz often spent several minutes standing by my cell door visiting with me while he was on duty. We talked about the war and Fritz wanted to know everything I could tell him about the United States.

It was through Fritz that I learned about the impending Allied invasion. On the actual day of June 6, 1944 when the Allies began landing troops in Normandy, he was almost breathless with excitement. We talked for quite some time that day. Apparently Fritz suspected Germany was losing the war. He was greatly concerned as to Germany's fate—and his own—after all the fighting was over.

After our talk that day about the invasion of Normandy, I lay on my bunk and thought about all the poor souls who were dying. It was a very emotional time for me. I prayed that the war would soon be over and all the suffering would come to an end.

From the time we escaped until we were returned to the camp stockade, we had heard nothing of how the war was going, so I eagerly anticipated each of my conversations with Fritz. He and I continued our talks for several more days. Then on June 13, he came in and told me that my three friends and I were to be returned to our barracks sometime around noon that day. Although the other *Kriegies* (POWs) knew we had been captured and returned to the camp stockade, there had been no communication between them and us, so excitement built up in anticipation of our release from solitary.

About noon Fritz came for me just as he had told me. He took me down to the office where I joined the other three. We were given a real strong warning about any future attempts to escape. The camp commander warned us we would never be returned to the camp under any circumstances. We might even be shot as spies.

BACK "HOME" —STALAG VI

After the German officer had completed his warnings and threats, he ordered the guards to take us to the compound and release us.

A large group of our guys were waiting for us. As soon as they saw us coming, they started yelling and cheering. Before long it seemed as if the whole compound of Kriegies had gathered around us. They were treating us like returning heroes. They shook our hands and congratulated us even though we had not succeeded in holding on to our freedom. We were overcome by all the attention and affection they heaped upon us.

From the night of our escape on March 11 until June 13, they had heard nothing about us. All sorts of rumors had circulated around the camp—some that we had made good our escape and others that we had been captured and shot as spies. They were eager for all the details about our experiences while we were out.

It took several days for all of us to catch up on our conversations and camp gossip. We four escapees wanted to know what took place when the German guards found out we had escaped. Our buddies told us

the whole compound had been ordered to stand for hours while the puzzled guards counted and recounted the prisoners.

The guards finally concluded that four POWs were missing, but they couldn't tell who had gotten out or how. It seemed to them that we must have disappeared into thin air. They caused trouble for everyone. They kept the prisoners standing in the snow for hours while guards tore up the barracks, searching for clues. After about a week they discovered the hole I had cut in the fence.

I don't recall making any special effort to conceal the hole but I had cut my way through on the diagonal. Because of the way the ditch deepened there at the hole, it was almost impossible to see the cut except at one particular point and even then, you almost had to be on your hands and knees and looking for it.

As a result of the hidden hole, I received praise and backslapping, which made me feel good. Also, since we four were the only ones ever to have escaped in the manner in which we had, we were suddenly considered experts. We were approached with all kinds of ideas about trying to get away. Although we had heard rumors that one or more Englishmen had managed to slip out of camp disguised as German guards, we never knew if it was true, and so we four maintained our expert status.

Although Patty Kerr—the British POW who had been so helpful in supplying us with the necessary wirecutters—was still in the compound, I don't recall seeing him after our return to camp. Our camp moved out in July and I never knew where he was sent.

I learned that although we four had escaped from the compound and had been returned unharmed, two other Kriegies who made an attempt on April 29th had been caught while still inside the compound. One of them had been killed.

As the story was related to me, George Walker and my old chess opponent, Ed Jurist, came up with a pretty good escape plan that went wrong because the guard on duty that night did not follow his usual routine.

Jurist and Walker had managed, with the help of several other Kriegies, to slip into the *Vorlager* where the Red Cross supplies were kept. Both men hid behind the large number of accumulated boxes. They planned to remain there until they felt it was safe to try to make their way up to the fence. Because the *Vorlager* was only a few feet from the guards' barracks, Jurist and Walker thought there would be less chance of their being seen. But the guard on post at that location kept walking back and forth instead of continuing around the fence perimeter. The two Kriegies should have stayed put.

They decided to try to make it to the fence but the guard spotted them. When he yelled at them, they stood up. The guard shot at them. Jurist and Walker fell back to the ground and lay there while the guard called for help. Other guards came running, bringing two large guard dogs. The dogs began to chew on the prisoners and Walker made the mistake of trying to get up. This time the guards shot him dead.

Jurist continued to lie still until several other guards came up and called the dogs off. Jurist figured the guards thought he was dead as a result of the rifle fire from the guard who had first discovered them. He cautiously let them know he was still alive. There was some confusion while the guards decided what to do.

The next morning the whole camp learned of the shooting.

The camp commandant, *Oberst* von Hoerbach, was in a state of rage: six Kriegies had attempted to escape in less than a month. He called the whole camp out on the grounds and told them, "Henceforth, anyone attempting to escape will be shot on the spot."

We four—LaMarca, Routon, Stapleton and I—were still loose at the time all that happened and there's no way of knowing if the commandant was aware of our recapture. Anyway, I am sure he must have been catching heat from the German High Command.

Ed Jurist gave me his account of the attempted escape and the shooting of Walker when I arrived back in camp. Ed and I wound up being placed in the same barracks and we would later make two escapes together.

Several weeks passed before the new wore off our return to camp and things began to return to everyday routine. You'd think the Germans would have known better than to throw possible conspirators together, but all four of us were placed in the same barracks with Ed Jurist and several other guys who were considered trouble-makers.

Things continued to rock along in the dull pattern of prison life, except for the constant fear of what would happen to you next. Scuttlebutt made its constant rounds about what was going on in camp and what the guards were going to do.

I suppose the practice drills the guards performed every few days worried me more than anything else. They circled the compound and set up machine-gun nests. Most of us were not certain the guards were not suddenly going to open fire upon the compound.

And they stepped up the number of their searches of the barracks. They entered the compound in force and ordered all the POWs to go to their barracks room and stand by their bunks. The guards then proceeded to search the rooms and the bunks.

They always seemed to look for extra bunk boards. Each bunk was supposed to have five boards, one-inch thick by six inches wide. If they found a board that was not the correct size they confiscated it. I suppose this was because prisoners trying to dig their way out of camp used the bunk boards to shore up their tunnels. I don't know of any successful escapes made from our camp by tunneling, but I heard of two or three attempts.

About this time, with the tide of war turning against them, the Germans began posting signs in some of the *Stalags*: "To All Prisoners of War! Escape from prison is no longer a game!"

For me, it never had been.

Once, when the guards searched our barracks, they found an extra board. The guard left our room to search the next one. He placed the board he had found right outside the door in the hall.

When the guard was out of sight, the owner of the extra board proceeded to go over and reclaim it. He placed the board under a table inside our room. After a few minutes the guard came out of the adjoining room and noticed the confiscated board was missing. He let out a loud shout and barged into our room to look for it.

The guard spotted the board at once. He grabbed it up and began beating the nearest POW. He struck the guy about five or six times across the back and buttocks as we all stood there and watched helplessly. The guy who had caused the beating in the first place went unscathed, but later he apologized to the poor soul who had received the beating.

I am sure the guards' frequent searches were also attempts to locate the small radio someone had smuggled into the compound. The radio was our only source of information about what was going on in the outside world. We hid it under the floor beneath the room's stove and used it sparingly.

Every few days we received word that our "reader," as he was called, would be coming to each barrack to give us the latest poop concerning the war and other pertinent information. We always took great precautions to see that he was not caught. As far as I know, none of the readers was ever caught nor was the radio found.

Somewhere around the first of July we learned our German captors might decide to move us because the camp was in danger of being overrun by the advancing Red Army. Most of us already knew about the Russians because we got news fairly regularly from the little radio. But we didn't have any way of predicting what the Germans planned to do with us. We all hoped that the Germans would abandon the camp and we would all be liberated.

This was not to be the case. On July 15, 1944 a large number of us were taken from the camp and placed on a train. We were taken to the port of Memel on the Baltic Sea coast of Lithuania. As Fate would have it, the four of us who had escaped together and had been almost inseparable were moved at this time to different camps. I was moved to *Stalag Luft* IV at or near Grosstychow. I did not learn until long after the war was over that LaMarca, Routon, and Stapleton were moved to *Stalag Luft* I at Barth, Germany.

After we were unloaded at the train station, our guards marched us to the Memel harbor where we boarded a fairly small ship named *Insterburg*. I never knew the total number, but there must have been several hundred of us. We were all forced down into the hold of the ship.

There were no mid-decks or anything on which to sit or lie so we perched along the inside of the hull, all along the ribs and bracing, like a flock of skinny birds. We were jammed so close together it was impossible to walk or move around.

Our only means of relieving ourselves was a bucket which was lowered through the hatch covers, passed around, and hauled back up by rope. Our only food— soup—was lowered the same way. We all hoped they were not using the same buckets for both purposes.

This trip along the coastline of Lithuania down to the German port of Swinemünde took about two days. We were all aware of the constant danger that the ship might be sunk by Allied aircraft. There would have been no way for any of us to save ourselves. There were no life preservers for us, and even if there had been, there would have been no way for us to get out of the hold of the ship.

We were greatly relieved when we finally reached the harbor of Swinemünde and we all crawled out of that cold, damp, packed hold that had been our enforced residence for two days.

While we were there in the harbor of Swinemünde we saw the last of Germany's great battleships, the *Scharnhorst*. Our guards unloaded us from our small ship and marched us to the train station. They handcuffed each of us to a fellow prisoner and loaded us onto the waiting boxcars under the watchful eyes of our *Kriegsmarine* guards.

The *Kriegsmarine* guards were quite young and seemed fairly friendly. Several of them were stationed in each boxcar to watch over us. They didn't seem particularly disturbed when a few of us managed to slip our skinny wrists out of the handcuffs; they simply ordered us to put them back on.

We were on the train for only about a day before we arrived at the town of Grosstychow. Our boxcars were broken off from the main train and shunted to a siding outside of town, known as Kiefheide. The siding was in a densely wooded area alongside a small dirt road leading to the camp where we were being sent.

THE RUN UP THE ROAD

The road was about three kilometers (about two miles) long and ran through the woods for the entire distance. We prisoners had no idea where or how far we were to be taken.

As soon as we were unloaded, we were ordered to line up about six or eight abreast there in the road. We were still handcuffed, making it almost impossible for a man to hold onto any of the pathetically small amount of gear that he was fortunate enough still to have.

We were all lined up waiting for orders to march out, when a German officer—we later learned he was *Hauptmann* Walter Pickhardt—began to talk to the young *Kriegsmarine* guards.

Pickhardt became very excited, yelling and shouting and gesturing toward us prisoners, telling the guards that we were the S.O.B.s and the bastards who had bombed their cities and killed their folks. Evidently he was trying to work them into a frenzy, for what purpose we could only guess. We saw many of the young guards turn from friendly to hostile as they listened to *Hauptmann* Pickhardt rave and rant for several minutes.

Finally the guards ordered us to move out at double-time or faster. Many of the guards were jabbing at us with their rifle bayonets and yelling and screaming at us to run faster and faster. We saw several excited guard dogs running alongside the column, leaping and biting at some of the prisoners.

As we ran further down the road we noticed machine guns set up at various points along the route. Incredibly, we saw photographers taking our pictures, documenting our forced run. I saw several civilians along the road, many of them yelling and shouting or jeering at us as we ran down the road. But I saw several of them crying, obviously very disturbed by what they saw taking place.

Although many of the young German marines were worked up, I saw several who were not engaging in any hostile actions. I remember seeing one of the marine guards take his bayonet off his rifle and throw it away. I often wondered what kind of excuse he offered for losing his bayonet. I hope somehow he was rewarded for his act of compassion.

As the run continued, many of the weak or injured prisoners began to drift back through the ranks to the rear of the column. Since we were handcuffed, two men together, it was a case of both men falling back. I remember seeing one of the guys who had only recently gotten out of the infirmary there at *Stalag Luft* VI. He was handcuffed to a very strong Jewish prisoner. I will never forget seeing them drift back toward the rear and hearing the strong one pleading with the weak one to try harder to keep up.

I was handcuffed to a strong buddy. Together we forged ahead, each giving strength to the other. We managed to keep away from the guard dogs and the soldiers' bayonets, even though we dropped and lost most of our gear.

I can't recall my handcuffed mate's first name. I think his last name was James and that he was from Rome, Georgia. He had been shot down a few weeks prior to our camp's evacuation. Fortunately for both of us he was uninjured and in good physical condition. I was relieved to know that he would be able to keep up and even help me if I should tire out or fall. I felt sure he would be a good man to have along in any kind of tough situation. The one we were now enduring was about as tough as I could imagine.

As soon as our column reached camp, *Stalag Luft* IV, we were all herded through the gates onto the compound grounds and ordered to sit down. The guards said if any of us stood up or made any movement, we would be shot on the spot.

We were all completely exhausted—many battered, bruised, and in shock. Mid-July weather in Germany is warm. After the three-kilometer run even those of us who were not injured were hot, hungry, and thirsty. My heart was pounding in my ears and I struggled to suck air into my lungs. My legs were weak and quivering, my ankles were swollen, and my feet were numb. We sat motionless for about an hour before we were broken into groups and ordered into our assigned barracks. We remained there for the rest of the day.

Many of our column who were injured eventually were carried to the camp hospital or infirmary. I don't know the exact number, but between twenty-five and thirty men were unable to go to their barracks until they received medical attention.

We later learned several dozen prisoners were bayoneted, beaten with clubs or rifle butts, and bitten by guard dogs. I think most of us were convinced *Hauptmann* Pickhardt had deliberately tried to provoke a mass escape so he could take photographs of our attempt and mow us down with machine guns he had placed along the road to camp. Any attempt on our part to break and run into the woods would have been a disaster for all of us.

The run to camp took place on July 18, 1944. I am sure not one of us who was forced to participate in it will ever forget.

I would like to mention that "The Run Up the Road" was brought up after the war and was to be presented to a War Crimes Tribunal. The case never went to trial due to lack of sufficient evidence. Although there was no prosecution, *Hauptmann* Pickhardt was arrested and later released. The Tribunal files refer to him as "The Mad Captain"—there were very few of us who would disagree.

We learned that the boat trip from Memel to Swinemünde also was brought before the War Crimes Tribunal but it too failed to go to trial for the same reason. All in all, some 1,600 accused German criminals were tried in military courts.

To continue my story, we were placed in our barracks and kept there for the rest of the day and all night without food. If we talked among ourselves at all it was in hushed voices as we tried to guess what else our captors had in store for us. The next morning we were permitted to resume our routines with roll call and a head-count.

Although we were the first to be forced to run from

the railroad siding to the camp, we were not the last. We saw several groups of prisoners brought to the camp in somewhat the same manner, although I am sure none of the runs was quite as severe. After a few weeks passed, this inhumane treatment stopped and things settled down to the customary cycles of prison life.

STALAG LUFT IV

O ur new camp, identified as *Stalag Luft* IV, was located near the town of Grosstychow, Pomerania, and twenty kilometers (about thirteen miles) southeast of Belgard. This camp was opened to American prisoners on May 12, 1944 and consisted of four compounds and a *Vorlager* with the German guards' barracks and the camp hospital.

The compounds, identified as A, B, C, and D, had ten to twelve wooden barracks designed to hold about 6,400 American and British POWs at capacity. The barracks were set about three feet up off the ground on blocks to prevent us from tunneling out.

Life in the new camp was essentially the same as it had been at *Stalag Luft* VI. The guards drilled constantly and frequently swooped into our barracks for unannounced searches.

Our food consisted mostly of kohlrabi stew mixed with what I am sure must have been horse meat. Our bread was dark and heavy and I am told it contained sawdust mixed with the coarse flour. Our coffee, when we had any, was an ersatz substance of parched barley. It was better than nothing, but not by much.

Fresh fruit and vegetables were nonexistent for us and probably, by that late in the war, pathetically scarce for the German civilian population as well. Aside from small quantities of salt there was never any seasoning. Pepper was withheld from us so we couldn't use it to desensitize the guard dogs.

We continued to receive Red Cross food packages. Usually two to four Kriegies split the packages. Most of the time we were belly-clinching hungry.

We spent our time daydreaming about which of our favorite foods we were going to keep stocked when we got home. We described to each other in tantalizing detail how we would jam the refrigerator full of all sorts of good foods, and we would never run out of anything. We would place the refrigerator just so—right beside our nice clean beds—so we wouldn't even have to get up to eat any time we wanted to.

Another thing we promised ourselves was that we would never have a door in our house that could be locked. We were going to insist that we have complete freedom of movement at all times. What fantasies you can conjure up when you have nothing better to do!

You may be surprised to know that sex usually was not a big topic of conversation among POWs. When you are undernourished, physically dirty, ill-clothed, infested, poorly housed, and confined a long way from home—well, there are other priorities.

We enjoyed some pastimes. We played all sorts of card games as well as chess and checkers. Anything of an unusual nature would bring the whole compound pouring out to watch or participate.

I vividly remember one such event.

A German Me-110 was flying acrobatics above our camp one day, rolling, diving, darting in and out of the clouds. Our whole camp turned out to crane our necks and watch the pilot perform—after all, we were flyers— and he really showed off to those of us on the ground.

Suddenly he came screaming out of the clouds in a steep dive and plunged straight to the ground less than a mile from where we all watched.

We heard a loud bang and saw a brilliant ball of fire. We reacted as if we had shot down the swastika-marked Messerschmitt ourselves. The whole compound exploded in loud cheering, shouting, and yelling.

I yelled as loudly as anyone but when I thought about it I really didn't understand our response at all. Most of us were there in prison camp because we had narrowly escaped death in the sky ourselves. My mind flashed back to the German pilots who could have shot me down as I dangled helplessly in my parachute above the water but had spared me.

I doubt if our German guards found anything unusual in our glee but they immediately hustled the whole compound back into the barracks. They kept us for some time before permitting us back outside.

On another occasion, the prisoners were standing around, idly watching a German electrician doing some repair work at the top of a high pole. The poor soul accidentally touched the wrong wire. He was electrocuted before our eyes. Once again the whole bunch of us Kriegies let out a whoop. Once again we were all herded back into our barracks for several hours.

I suppose the situation we found ourselves in created such a heartless lack of regard for our fellowman.

Maybe we simply believed that was the way we were supposed to react.

Another tragedy—which brought about an altogether different reaction—occurred during a severe thunderstorm. Lightning struck a tent occupied by several British POWs, killing one of them and injuring several others. Ironically the dead prisoner had been shot down in early September 1939 on the first day of England's entry into the war. He had been a prisoner for almost five years. He'd lived and suffered through so much and then to be killed by a random act of Nature. The whole camp mourned his death for days.

Life went on. We continued to drag through our daily existence in camp. We still had our secret radio; every few days our POW grapevine brought us up to date on the progress of the war. We knew that once again the Russian army was getting close to our camp. We hoped if our German captors didn't march us out, the advancing Russians might overrun the camp and liberate us.

Freedom was not to be won so easily. Once more the German commandant gave instructions for the camp to prepare for evacuation.

BLACK MARCH

About February 6, 1945 we were herded out to make what became known as the Black March on the Shoe Leather Express back toward the heart of Germany. Actually the term was inaccurate—by that time precious few of us had any shoe leather left.

Before we evacuated *Stalag Luft* VI, I had been in the same barracks with Ed Jurist. He was of Russian descent; he spoke Russian and some French. He and I became good friends, despite the fact that I always beat him at chess.

Ed and I both were close enough to two other POWs that we felt safe in sharing our thoughts about escaping from the German camp. They were Robert Rector and Norris T. (Tex) Reynolds. Both were glad to be included in our plans. Rector was from Mississippi and was about two or three years younger than I was. He was still in good health and physical condition and didn't want any more of the forced march.

Reynolds, from Jacksboro, Texas was always a gambler anyway so he was willing to cast his lot with us. He was in good condition and well able to make the plan work. Tex was on his second tour of duty. He had flown in the South Pacific Theater and had married an Australian girl. Like the rest of us, he didn't relish any more of the forced marches and hardships we knew were ahead if we stayed with the entire group.

Anyway, we had already given up hopes of being abandoned by the retreating German army or being overrun by the advancing Red Army. We all agreed: we would make our move at the first opportunity.

The bitter weather as well as our own dwindling physical stamina fueled our determination to get away from the march.

February in my Central Texas home is almost spring. February in Germany is still clinched in the grip of winter. Every day we were forced to march in ice and snow. We lacked the nourishment of adequate food and felt our strength draining from us. Our shoes were in tatters and our feet were so cold and painful we could barely remain upright. We knew if we did not escape soon we would be unable to keep up with the other marchers—much less make our break for freedom.

At night during our forced march the guards kept us in large barns selected along our route. They herded us inside the barn and then posted guards around the outside. The whole bunch of us would be left there without light, food or bedding until time to move out the next morning.

When morning came, the guards ordered all of us out of the barn. Several of them entered and prodded with pitchforks to see if anyone was trying to hide. I don't recall any head counts during the march but after watching how thoroughly those guards used their pitchforks no one was willing to risk hiding in the hay.

On the fourth day out, Jurist and I and our two buddies, Rector and Reynolds, decided it was now or never. We had to escape! Late that evening the guards selected a rambling wooden barn for us to spend the night in. We studied every detail of the layout.

We noticed several small sheds and some pigpens on the backside of the barn. We figured the guards couldn't patrol any closer than twenty-five or thirty feet of the barn because of the attached sheds and pens. As soon as we entered the barn we crept to the back wall. We settled down to wait and to make further observations.

Through a crack in the barn wall we could see the guard was doing exactly as we had hoped. He was not likely to see or hear us when we broke through the barn wall. We figured once we made it out to the pigpens, we could lie low until the guard passed. Then we'd scramble the short distance to the protection of the woods. We observed the guards carefully, waiting for our chance.

ESCAPE NUMBER THREE

By the time darkness fell we had figured out their routine. We started to work on the barn boards. The boards were loose enough to pry apart easily. In minutes we pushed two of them open at the bottom.

One after another the four of us bellied through the narrow opening and into the adjacent pigpen and pitch-dark shed. We had no trouble concealing ourselves but we waited tensely until the guard made his rounds and walked away from us. Moving as quickly and quietly as possible we slid through the fence surrounding the pigpen. We crawled on our hands and knees toward the cover of the nearby woods. The darkness of night and the splotches of ice and snow on contrasting dark ground made good cover for us. We reached the woods without detection.

We had decided our safest bet was to double back to the camp we had just vacated. We gambled that it was now unoccupied. We figured we'd hide out there and wait for the Russian army to overrun the camp. Then we would be free.

We walked most of that first night in the direction of the old camp. Sometime before daylight we hid in a small growth of trees and tried to get some sleep. Snow fell on us and it was bitterly cold. We had no packs or bedding—only the clothes on our backs. We were almost freezing. We lay there in the snow, each taking turns trying to keep warm by sandwiching between the other men. We spent a miserable two or three hours in this restless fashion. As soon as it was full daylight we continued in the direction of our abandoned camp.

During the first two escapes our idea had been to stay out of sight. That was now impossible.

Heavy pedestrian and truck traffic hurried along glutted roads. Fortunately no one seemed particularly interested in the four of us. My feet were so sore and swollen I could hardly stand, much less walk. Luckily we were able to catch a ride with a German army truck going in our direction. Jurist, with his fluent German, told the soldier we were trying to return to our prison camp. He was blithely happy to help us along the way.

The truck driver dropped us off in the vicinity of Belgard where we spent the night in a sort of canteen set up for refugees and army personnel. Everyone seemed in a state of near panic. They couldn't have cared less who we were or where we were going. No one asked to see our identification or passes—which was a good thing because we didn't have any.

When morning came we left immediately in the direction of our old camp and arrived there late in the afternoon. I never thought a *Stalag* would look so good to us. Our plan had worked perfectly! We expected to find the camp vacant and—sure enough—we saw there were no guards in the towers or at the gates. Confidently we strode right into the camp.

PRISONERS' SHUFFLE

We immediately found ourselves surrounded by a couple of dozen German soldiers pointing their rifles at us.

Much to our dismay, we realized the German army once more occupied the camp.

We stood there stupidly for a moment before we reacted and tried to duck out of sight. If the guards were surprised to see us run right up to them, they still had the presence of mind to capture us and place us in the compound—this time filled with Russian and Polish POWs.

Most of these poor souls had been marched into this camp from other camps even closer to the Russian front. They were really in pitiful shape. Clearly the Germans were using the camp as a layover for prisoners they were moving away from the approaching Red Army. We spent the night there in the camp. Early the next morning the whole camp moved out.

Again we were unwillingly heading deeper into the Fatherland, only this time we were just four sad-sack American GIs among several hundred Russian and Polish prisoners. The Germans considered them less than dirt. The guards mistreated and beat stragglers. We knew we could expect no mercy if any of us should fall behind.

Little communication was possible among us but little was needed. We made up our minds we would try once more to escape as soon as we could. We agreed on a plan of sorts.

We were in worse shape than when we had first marched away from the camp. Our blistered feet were swollen. We dared not take off our ragged shoes for fear of not being able to get them back on. We were barely able to drag along, doing what we called the "prisoners' shuffle." Somehow we managed to keep up with the rest of the marchers. We stuck close to one another so we could quickly reach the side of a buddy who needed help.

We were determined to keep going until our captors put us up in some barn or other shelter for the night. Then we would break away from the march.

We were nearing the town of Treptow as night approached. As we had hoped, our guards located a large barn and jammed us all in together. The Germans didn't bother to post a guard at the rear of the barn. We quickly realized they were not as alert as usual. Maybe they didn't believe any of us had the strength or spirit left to try to escape from the barn.

As soon as we were shut inside we made our way to the rear wall and started searching for loose boards or any way out. We located a section of rotten boards and pried them loose.

The other prisoners silently watched us. They made no effort to interfere, nor did they show any desire to escape with us.

ESCAPE NUMBER FOUR

As soon as things seemed to quiet down, all four of us slipped through the opening in the wall. We crawled on our hands and knees toward the forest several hundred feet away. Once we were well into the woods we stood up and walked for about a mile or more in the direction of the approaching Russian forces.

We had traveled only an hour or so away from the barn. We were completely worn out before we came to a small stand of planted pine or fir trees. We made our way into them for several hundred feet and decided to try to get some sleep. We felt sure that even if our captors missed us, they wouldn't waste time looking for us. We believed the Germans were much more interested in getting themselves and the main body of their prisoners as far away from the advancing Red Army as possible.

The snow continued to fall. We lay there in between the rows of slender trees, burrowed into the scant ground cover of needles and snow, shaking and shivering and huddled together in a desperate effort to keep from freezing to death in our sleep. We remained there in the trees, dozing but alert, until shortly after daylight.

About the time we thought it was safe to leave the thin protection of trees, we heard sounds of someone chopping wood not too far from where we crouched. We got down on our hands and knees and crawled to the edge of our cover nearest the sound.

We were able to make out five men. From what we could see, we guessed them to be four Frenchmen and an old German civilian.

We waited until we noticed one of them glance in our direction. Then we waved, caught his attention, and motioned for him to come to where we were hiding. As soon as he got close enough, we explained we were Americans, we had escaped from the march, and we were hungry.

"Can you help us?" we asked.

The guy was very friendly. He seemed to understand us. He said his name was René and he and ten other French prisoners were working in a big German military hospital not very far from Treptow. They were out cutting firewood for the hospital and the old German civilian was their boss. René spoke enough English to tell us to wait there while he went back to talk to his companions.

René huddled a few minutes with the rest of the Frenchmen and the old German. He turned and motioned for us to come over to them. We didn't know what kind of story he spun for the old German, but we were told we could accompany them back to the hospital. René assured us we would be safe.

As soon as the work detail completed their wood-gathering, we helped them load the kindling on a small cart. We all headed in the direction of the hospital. Could we really get away with hiding right under the Germans' noses? When we got to the hospital grounds, we acted as if we belonged there. We walked right past the German soldiers and officers on our way to the Frenchmen's quarters.

René lead us to an entrance with stairs leading to the basement of the hospital. All eleven of the Frenchmen lived there in a large room and were permitted to have free run of the place. We supposed that the Germans felt it was unnecessary to guard the French—they had no place to escape to as France, for the most part, was still under German control. Anyway, the Frenchmen had it pretty good where they were, all things considered. They took care of all kinds of maintenance around the hospital and helped out with cooking. They managed to live rather well, what with all they could steal from the hospital supplies. No real guard was posted over them.

As soon as we got through with our initial introductions and excitement, they prepared us a good solid meal of ham, canned green beans, and carrots—with pepper and salt to season the food to our taste. Best of all there was some fresh French bread with butter. This was the first white bread any of us had eaten since being shot down. We even had some wine to go with our meal.

While we were relishing this feast we laughed and said we sure hoped we weren't depriving some poor, hard-working German SS trooper or Gestapo agent of his ration of white bread.

Boy, did we ever enjoy that meal! And even better, we had a good long night's sleep.

The next morning the Frenchmen told us we could stay there as long as we wanted to. They showed us several hiding places if for any reason the Germans decided to search the basement. They told us to crawl back among the pipes running through small tunnels under the hospital. I recall only once or twice we had to scramble for cover during the two weeks we stayed there.

The Frenchmen had a radio and we were able to keep up with the news.

Unlike the radio we had back in the *Stalag Lufts*, this was a regular commercial model and the French didn't seem too concerned about trying to conceal it. I suppose they were so used to the German guards' routine that they felt fairly safe. Most of the news reports were in German and many of the Frenchmen were able to understand it very well.

We felt certain the hospital would be evacuated soon. Sure enough, within a week or ten days, the French alerted us that preparations were underway for the hospital unit to move out.

The Frenchmen were very busy as their labor was being used in making preparations for the abandonment of the hospital. They kept us filled in to what was happening, such as the evacuation of the patients and the moving of supplies and equipment. Most of the time during the evacuation we stayed hidden back in the pipe tunnels. We didn't want to take a chance on being found and once again put on a forced march, even with German hospital patients.

In a couple of days we found the whole place was empty except for us and the eleven Frenchmen, whom the Germans made no effort to take with them. In their haste to evacuate they left nearly all their supplies behind.

We spent some time exploring the deserted camp but we continued to stay in the hospital basement as we believed it was safer than being above ground. We still didn't know if the Germans would be coming back or to what use they might want to put the hospital.

The French knew exactly where the wine cellar was located as well as the food supply room. What a feast we had that first day or two after the evacuation! In their haste the Germans had left much of their food supply consisting of canned pork and poultry, several cheeses, and an assortment of other canned goods. It might not have been enough to feed an army but it was abundant for our needs. The Frenchmen were really good cooks—they were eager to put their talents to good use and we four were appreciative trenchermen.

But our basement paradise was to last only a few days. Then things started to get grim.

WHAT NOW?

We could hear the sound of gunfire and bombings and we knew a great deal of fighting raged all around us.

For two days we listened to sounds of battle. We remained hidden in the basement, not daring to stick our heads out for fear of being shot. Sometime around the third or fourth day, we heard the clanking of an approaching tank. We peered out the basement windows and saw a large Russian tank moving through the hospital grounds.

We saw several Russian soldiers running behind the tank and we felt confident the Russians were in control of the area. We didn't dare come out of our basement yet, but shortly after the tank passed through the grounds we saw a lone Russian soldier walking along the street in front of our hiding place. A German girl was walking with him. We saw they were coming toward the hospital entrance, so we decided we'd better make our presence known.

We came up from the basement. When the Russian and the girl got to the hospital entrance we called out to them. We stepped outside with our hands in the air. For an anxious moment we didn't know whether the guy was going to shoot us or not. Evidently he recognized the words *"Amerikanets"* and *"tovarishch,"* because he motioned for us to approach him.

Jurist was able to speak to him in Russian. He learned the town of Treptow had been taken and was now under Russian control. The Russian assured Jurist it was safe for us to go into Treptow, but we still heard gunfire coming from the direction of the town. We decided we'd be safer remaining at the hospital a while longer.

The next day Tex Reynolds and I could stand it no longer. We decided to go to Treptow and see if we could find some help getting back to our own forces. We picked out a couple of abandoned bicycles, filled our canteens with the best cognac we could find in the hospital wine cellar, and started pedaling into town.

Obviously control of the town still was being contested. We soon realized we'd made a big mistake. Fighter planes strafed the town and we heard shooting. We saw dead bodies lying in rubble all along the streets or half-hanging out of windows.

We were about ready to turn and race back to the safety of the hospital when we spotted a couple of Russian soldiers inside a small house near us. We decided to check with them. Maybe they could tell us which way to go.

When we reached the house, we saw both Russians were so drunk they could hardly stand. They were drinking some sort of alcoholic beverage from a large clear glass jug. They grabbed their rifles when they saw us approach. We wasted no time in telling them we were Americans.

As soon as we said those magic words, both soldiers threw their arms around us and shouted "*Americanets tovarishch*," or words to that effect. They embraced us and kissed our cheeks.

They offered us some of the stuff they were drinking from the glass jug but we refused. I suppose we might have tried to drink from their jug to be polite but it looked vile and probably lethal. The glass jug itself was covered with dust and cobwebs and the pale yellowish liquid had what appeared to be a small piece of corn cob floating in it. At that time of my life I might have tried almost anything, but I couldn't bring myself to taste that concoction, whatever it was.

We needed Jurist along—with his command of the language he could have thrown in some smooth diplomatic phrases. All I could do was keep repeating, "*Nyet, nyet.*" Our curt refusal made them angry. Apparently they took our rejection as a personal—or perhaps even international—insult. Again they demanded to know who we were and again we identified ourselves as Americans. They kept insisting that we drink with them and we kept refusing. Our own cognac was smooth as parachute silk and we even offered them a drink of it, but they still wanted us to drink some of the mystery juice from their jug.

I noticed an old German couple cowering in a corner of the house. From their frightened expressions I figured they must have thought we'd all be shot if we continued to refuse to drink. I must admit we were beginning to fear the same fate.

About that time I had such a crazy idea that it's with some reluctance I tell you what happened next. It all seemed so much like a skit from some sort of amateur comedy play.

Anyway, for reasons I will never figure out, I suddenly snapped to full attention and shouted "Ten-HUT!" in a loud commanding voice. The two Russian soldiers, drunk as they were, responded automatically. They struggled to straighten themselves and salute as best they could. Without waiting around to exchange further military courtesies, Tex and I wheeled around and marched briskly to our bicycles.

We mounted our bikes. Without looking back we made a hasty retreat out of town in the direction of the hospital. I don't know how long those two drunk soldiers stood there at attention, but I hope it was long enough for the old German couple to slip away from them.

I suppose we were about half way back to our hospital hideout and still complimenting ourselves on not getting shot, bombed or poisoned, when the road we were traveling broke out of the woods into open country.

Tex and I were about to ride our bikes out into the open when we looked to our right and saw, only a hundred yards or so away, a small group of mounted soldiers heading in our direction.

We looked at each other and, without exchanging a word, agreed that we would stop right where we were and wait for the riders to pass in front of us. We figured if we tried to hide or turn back toward town that the soldiers would probably think the worst and take after us. We stepped off our bikes and stood there, waiting and watching.

That was some parade that passed not a hundred feet in front of us. The men were all wearing quilted snowsuits that at one time had been white but now were a dismal greasy gray color. They were all very short and had round faces with almond-shaped eyes. Most of them wore long, black, drooping handlebar mustaches. I don't think I have ever seen, before or since, a more hard-bitten lot.

I knew they were Mongolians—I recognized them from pictures and movies I had seen. The thought raced through my head that these men were descendants of Genghis Khan's Mongol hordes who had overrun Eastern Europe early in the thirteenth century. I had read about them in my history books. All I could think of was that it must have been one hell of a bad experience. Their mounts were small, sturdy white ponies with long, shaggy hair. I don't think they were much larger than the Shetland ponies we are familiar with in the States.

Some of the ponies were dragging along four or five of what we took to be water-cooled machine guns. There must have been at least a hundred men in this group and what seemed so unusual was that they were not making any noise at all—no singing, yelling or anything, just plodding silently along.

Tex and I were less than a hundred feet away, staring at them. They must have seen us but they gave us no notice or concern whatsoever and continued on past. I guess they realized a couple of unarmed, escaped

American POWs on "liberated" bicycles were no threat to them. They were the meanest, toughest looking bunch you could ever imagine. I was glad they were on our side but I felt that I now had a better understanding of why the young German soldiers we had talked with back in Königsberg seemed desperate to be away from the Russian battlefront.

Tex and I both wondered where that bunch was headed but we sure didn't have any desire to ask. We decided it was safe to continue on our way to the hospital after the group had moved on past us at least two or three hundred yards. We could hardly believe that we hadn't been questioned or searched or anything. I know that if we had been asked to share a drink with any of them, we both simply would have asked, "How much?"

With a sigh of relief, we mounted our bikes and headed once more toward the hospital.

When we arrived back at the hospital, we found things exactly as we had left them. Jurist and Rector were still there. So were the eleven Frenchmen. I guess they had mixed reactions: they were glad to see us but sorry we didn't make it. Tex and I decided we might as well stay around with the others a couple more days and enjoy all the French cooking and good wine and cognac.

About the third day, Tex Reynolds got restless and decided he wanted to risk going back to Treptow. "I'll gamble on it," he said. We tried to convince him to stay a little longer, but he took off on his bike.

Ed Jurist, Bob Rector, and I wasted a couple more days and then we too said goodby to our French friends. We rode off on the bicycles we had found abandoned at the hospital.

We had decided against going toward Treptow. Instead we planned on going back toward Russia. We rode our bicycles for several days and passed on the outskirts of what remained of Warsaw. The Polish capital city had been occupied by the Germans since 1939 and now showed almost complete destruction. Large numbers of refugees wandered around the countryside. The sight was pitiful. Most of the people had only the clothing on their backs. The weather was severe and snow fell constantly. The sick and wounded were everywhere and it seemed to me no one made an effort to take care of any of them.

I recall one incident in particular when we saw a large group of refugees out in the middle of a field. As we passed by, they motioned us to come over. We saw a very old woman lying on her back in the snow. I gave her a drink of cognac from my canteen and we continued on our way. There was nothing more we could do.

As we continued on our way, we began to have contact with a number of Russian army units and learned there was supposed to be a train going back toward Odessa, and one or two of the freight cars were loaded with liberated prisoners.

Russian soldiers were everywhere. I don't think I have ever seen any group of soldiers who enjoyed shooting and drinking as much as the Russians. I would like to say that in all our contacts with Russian soldiers we were treated with great affection and emotion. They hugged us and kissed our cheeks. They left no doubts in our minds that they accepted us as comrades in arms.

It is with some reluctance that I relate the demise of my much-beloved black trousers—the ones I traded from our good Lithuanian friend.

We three—Reynolds was still off by himself some-where—had stopped to spend the night in a large house occupied by a number of Russian officers. They were having a party and insisted that we join them.

The stuff they were drinking must have been pure white lightning and they drank it by the cupful. Ed Ju-rist, our gracious translator, matched the Russians toast for toast. We saluted the health of Premier Josef Stalin and President Roosevelt and Prime Minister Winston Churchill and everyone else on down the ranks. Our generous hosts kept pouring the stuff to us and we didn't resist as hard as we should have. Before long we three inexperienced Americans were over-dosed. I can hazily recall that I either found or was led to a bed. I immedi-ately sprawled across it and went to sleep or passed out.

When I awoke the next morning I found that some-time during the night someone—surely not I!—had thrown up everything but their socks all over my beau-tiful black trousers.

I had no choice but to discard them. I had no way of cleaning them and I sure as heck couldn't continue to wear them. With great reluctance I pulled them off, at the same time swearing to myself I'd never again touch a drop of that Russian liquor that looked like water and had the lethal impact of an eighty-eight.

The removal of the smelly black trousers left me with only two layers of trousers plus my longhandle under-wear but not smelling a whole lot better.

As well as I remember my two buddies didn't fare much better than I did. After we reduced our heads back down to cap size we were ready to bid our hospitable Russian hosts farewell and continue on our way.

RANK HAS ITS PRIVILEGES

We immediately set our course for the town where the train to Odessa was expected to arrive.

Before we had left the hospital at Treptow, we had promoted ourselves to the army rank of captains. We figured the Russian forces might give officers better treatment. Our hunch had proved to be correct, as evidenced by our generous Russian hosts the night before. But now that we were going to be on a train bound for Odessa, we decided we'd better bust ourselves back to our own ranks—I think we were all sergeants.

We arrived in the small town—I don't recall the name—in the middle of the afternoon and learned the train would be pulling into the station sometime later that day.

We heard that an American captain was in charge of the two boxcars of prisoners. That sounded good to us—the quicker we were back under American command the safer and happier we'd feel. Shortly before dark the train pulled into the station. The POWs who had gathered there to board the train were on hand to greet its arrival.

Left to right, Robert Rector, an unknown young Russian soldier, and the author, Harvey Gann. The escapees were making their way toward Odessa in early April 1945. Ed Jurist took the picture with a camera found in an abandoned German home.

Ed Jurist takes his turn in front of the camera, wearing the Russian soldier's hat.

The unkown Russian soldier posed for his new ex-Kriegie friends.

The author, Harvey E. ("Moe") Gann.

Robert Rector, one of the Kriegies who escaped from the Black March with the author.

When the three of us—Jurist, Rector and I—arrived in town we met an American first lieutenant who had been a POW for only two or three weeks before his release. He was still going by the book. He had no idea how we long-timers had learned to scheme and connive to keep ourselves alive. We saw right away that he was very rank-conscious and thought we should all go around saluting him. We couldn't have cared less about his rank, but we did get a big laugh when he ran up to greet the American captain who stepped off the train.

The lieutenant threw the captain a snappy salute and made it known that he was awaiting further instructions. The "captain," in the person of none other than Staff Sergeant Norris T. Reynolds, obviously hadn't expected this development.

He saw the three of us standing there, choking back our laughter as we realized what had happened. Tex excused himself from the lieutenant and came over to where we were waiting. Keeping up the charade we threw him stiff, correct salutes. Reynolds didn't see the situation as being all that comical. He was concerned that the Russians might discover his real rank. No telling how they might react if they believed they had been fooled.

His first words were, "Moe, what in the hell am I going to do?"

"Just play it cool and keep up the act," I replied. "I don't see any way the Russians will know the difference unless you tell them."

Reynolds' next question was a little more complicated. "Well, what in hell am I going to do about that shave-tail? He thinks I'm a real captain. He's been saluting me all over the place."

"You better cut him in on your act," I advised. "I don't think he has any choice but to go along with you, at least till we get to our own military people in Odessa."

My answer to Tex's dilemma seemed to satisfy him and, with a sigh of relief, he trotted back to inform the lieutenant of his impersonation.

The news upset the lieutenant but he had to play along. He was no more eager than we were to cause a problem with the Russians. Anyway, we got a big kick out of seeing the very formal Russian officers passing information to Captain Reynolds, who then passed it on down through his first lieutenant.

The train remained there in the small town for two more days. Then we were put aboard the boxcars and headed toward Odessa. All along the way I noticed that Russian women were running the trains, clearing the rubble, and doing all the hard, physical work.

The weather was still bitterly cold and it snowed on us almost every day. Even though we were on board a train and under control of the Russian army, we were still ill-fed and suffering constantly from the cold. The thought of complaining never entered our minds, as you can hardly imagine the sad state of the poor people we saw along the way. The whole countryside had suffered from the scorched earth policy of both the Russian and German armies as they fought back and forth for control of the land.

We passed through small villages that were hardly more than piles of rubble. The civilians who watched us move through were all old and worn-out looking, with not much more than rags on their backs. Nothing but complete destruction as far as the eye could see. This was the way it was all the way to Odessa.

We finally arrived in Odessa on April 3, 1945. We American prisoners were met by a U.S. Military Mission sent there to arrange for our transportation and return to the States. The official translators, both Russian and American, and many of the other processors were women in uniform.

The very first thing the Military Mission did for us was to arrange for delousing. Then we were issued new clothing of regular army uniforms and shoes. At last I was able to shed my collection of trousers. Boy, did we ever feel good! We were assigned to temporary quarters where we were to remain until our transportation back to the States could be arranged.

Throughout this narrative I've used the term "Russia" but I should have said the Union of Soviet Socialist Republics—fifteen or so nations of which Russia was the largest. Odessa was in the Ukrainian People's Republic. The Mongols we had seen were probably from the Mongolian People's Republic.

In Odessa I was given a 1945 Soviet calendar, printed in English. It wasn't a wall or desk calendar. It was bound like a book with a black embossed cover with the numerals 1945 in red and looked for all the world like a college or large high school annual. Each page had information about a Soviet hero or battle or a famous author or poet.

The page about "Heroic Odessa" told how Odessa had been a famous seaport and industrial city with a population of over 600,000 before the war. In October 1941 the Germans took the city after terrible fighting and held it for thirty months. The Russians, or Ukrainians, took Odessa back on April 10, 1944—almost exactly a year before we ex-POWs straggled in. The battle for Odessa has been described as a turning point in the European war. Germany suffered heavy casualties in the fighting and in the retreat. German civilians who had settled in various German-occupied areas began streaming back to their original homes.

I know the calendar was issued as Soviet propaganda but I enjoyed reading it and it is still one of my treasured possessions.

When we arrived in Odessa, we each were issued an "Identity Card for Ex-Prisoners of War." It was a slip of plain typing paper, only a little larger than a dollar bill, with my name, rank, and serial number, dated 4-3-45 Odessa. Within a circle, like a postmark, were the words: "U.S. Military Mission." The city was filled with people of all nationalities; we were required always to have our passes and be ready to show them on demand.

We were surprised at the behavior of the American Military Mission personnel. They were very secretive

Identity card front and back

and advised us not to talk to any of the Russian army officers. We were forbidden to leave the complex where we were lodged. The strict precautions almost made us feel we were still in a hostile camp instead of with our friends.

All during the war we had thought of the Russians as America's allies. Most of the Russians we had anything to do with grabbed us, hugged us, and shouted "*Amerikanets.*" You would have thought we were all long-lost brothers.

Evidently with the certain defeat of our common enemy—Germany—the political picture changed somewhere up the line. To us this was a complete turn-around from the good will we'd enjoyed from Russian soldiers since our escape. We endured the strained situation for several days and then we were placed aboard an American merchant marine ship that had arrived in the harbor of Odessa.

Once on board the ship we were treated in an altogether different manner. The ship's crew were friendly but we were still forbidden to go ashore.

We'd been prisoners too long to allow our new freedom to be restricted for reasons we couldn't understand. We immediately made plans to grant ourselves shore leave.

I happened to make friends with one of the ship's radio operators. He was about my size so I borrowed one of his uniforms. I thought I really looked sharp in his navy blue trousers, white shirt, and billed cap. To top all this off I wore his full-length dark blue topcoat. Unless someone had asked me for an identification picture, there was no way to tell I wasn't a regular crew member. Jurist and Rector did the same thing and we all went ashore dressed as sailors. This was strictly against regulations but it seemed like a fool-proof idea at the time. At least we would be able to say we had visited a few places in the Ukrainian city of Odessa.

The city and its civilian population had suffered horribly at the hands of the German army. Many buildings had been destroyed. Much of what remained standing had been badly damaged. Here again we saw crews of Russian women working. Russian women did all kinds of jobs during the war—they were nurses, medics, snipers, and fighter pilots.

After a few days our ship left Odessa and sailed across to Poeti. This was just a small port town. I remember seeing several Russian submarines lying at anchor in the harbor.

The first night we were in port, Jurist, Rector, and I again arranged to borrow our friendly crew members' uniforms. Once more we slipped ashore.

While we were walking around the town Jurist, our handy translator, learned there was a nice dance place located on the far side of the town. We decided to go there and check it out.

Since the place was quite a way from the harbor, we expected to be the only Americans there. There were a number of good-looking Russian girls there, but we spent our time talking and drinking with the Russian soldiers and sailors. The Russians were buying nearly all of the drinks. We had only a few dollars that our good merchant marine friends had given us. I guess that is why we didn't try our luck with the women since we had no money to buy them drinks. We did look at them on the sly however.

We spent an hour or so there by ourselves. Then several of the American ship's real crew came in the front door. They joined us at our table as if we were old shipmates. We had to share the limelight with them but that was only fair since we were wearing uniforms borrowed from them.

I never could recall how it happened, but for some reason the ship's first mate and I got into a heated argument. I think it was over a Russian cap, or something equally silly. We wound up throwing punches and having a big fight right there in the place. I recall waiters running around frantically trying to move furniture and potted plants out of our way while this guy and I rolled around on the floor. By the time the rest of our bunch finally got us separated, the first mate and I each had a black eye for our efforts.

When the dust settled and things returned to normal we left the place and started back to the ship. I remember walking along the dock where the submarines were anchored. We were loudly singing a Russian song called "Moscow Nights" or something like that. I remembered hearing the Russian POW honey-bucket crew sing the song while they were emptying the latrine in our compound.

The song originated during the war and was full of longing to return home. As for what that song meant to Russian soldiers, I guess it was about the same as "Lili Marlene" to some of the rest of us.

Our rendition wouldn't have filled a concert hall with eager music lovers but the night was beautiful and our singing was considerably improved by the clear, damp seaport air. We'd had more than enough to drink and I was astonished to discover not only that I could sing in Russian—a language I couldn't speak—but also that I had a passable bass voice.

Above all, we were free and on our way home.

We finally boarded our ship for the night and I don't recall our making any more shore leaves while we were there. I stuck close to my bunk and kept a very low profile for several days. I was sure the first mate would be sporting a black eye the mirror image of mine. I didn't want to take any chances he might try to pull rank on me or throw me in the brig or whatever he could do. After all, it was his ship.

After a few days in Poeti, the ship was ready to sail again. We headed down through the Black Sea in the direction of the Straits of Dardanelles and the Port of Istanbul.

While we were still onboard ship in the Black Sea and shortly after we had sailed from Poeti, we heard of the death of President Roosevelt on April 12, 1945. The ship's captain broadcast to the whole ship that Roosevelt had died and that Harry Truman was now president of the United States. The whole bunch of us were saddened and concerned as to what this would do to the war effort. We felt sure that the war with Germany was about over, but there still remained Japan in the Pacific and we knew that a great deal of fighting still lay ahead.

The voyage was rather uneventful except that the captain of the ship wanted us POWs to stand watch. On my first turn at watch I was as nervous as I'd been before any escape attempt. This time the lives of all the men aboard plus the safety of the ship itself depended on my alertness.

I spotted a dark, bobbing mass and called out in a loud voice, "A floating mine on the port side!"

Several members of the ship's crew came scrambling out on deck and the crew manning the deck gun swung their weapon in the direction that I was pointing. I looked again and realized the "mine" that I had spotted was actually a school of porpoises, jumping playfully in and out of the waves. It had sure looked real to me! I was embarrassed by my mistake but the crew assured me that it was better to give a false alert than to go to sleep on watch.

When we reached the port of Istanbul, we asked to be transferred to another ship. We objected to standing watch because most of us ex-POWs were still in very poor physical condition and hardly able to function, let alone pull watch duty. There happened to be a troop ship, the *Peter Minuet*, in the harbor in Istanbul and all the American POWs were transferred aboard her.

I recall how beautiful the city of Istanbul was and how clear and blue the water in the harbor was. From our ship we could see a number of minarets scattered around the harbor and five times a day we heard a muezzin call the Moslem faithful to prayer. Although we remained in the port of Istanbul for two or three days, we never had an opportunity to go ashore. Only a few of the ship's officers went ashore while we were in Istanbul. None of the ship's regular crew went ashore so none of us ex-POWs had a chance to pull our masquerade act again.

A delegation from the Red Cross, some of them women, came aboard the ship and handed out a number of small gifts, including pairs of blue pajamas. We all thought it was kind of funny, having those nice new blue PJs after the months on end we had slept in all our clothes.

On the *Peter Minuet* we found a fairly large number of German POWs. There must have been about two hundred or more of them. They had sleeping quarters below deck, but there was a large barbed-wire enclosure amid-ship and that is where they liked to spend much of their daylight hours. Many of them spoke fairly good English and we knew a little German by then so we could carry on a conversation and exchange war stories. We spent a great deal of time talking to them. They all seemed happy to be headed to the United States—quite different from the way I felt when I had been captured and knew I was headed for Germany. They were surprised to learn we were ex-POWs of the Fatherland and that, for the most part, we didn't hold any grudges against them.

We remained in the Istanbul harbor a few days and once more resumed our journey home. We learned the ship was scheduled to dock in the United States at the port of Newport News, Virginia but we were given no definite date or time. For several days we sailed along with no great concern for enemy subs or aircraft although a continuous watch was set and the ship's guns were manned constantly.

I think the most excitement on the whole crossing resulted from a friendly wrestling match Ed Jurist and I had on about the third day at sea. I threw a headlock on Jurist and he thrashed around trying to get loose. Suddenly he went limp. My hold had hit something in his neck he'd hurt when he'd bailed out over Germany. I was scared to death. I thought, *Here's my good buddy on his way home at last from German prisons, and I've broken his neck.* I was convinced that even if he lived he'd be paralyzed for life.

The ship's doctor thought Jurist should be moved to a shore hospital immediately, and the *Endicott*, a U.S.

destroyer, was called to do the job. While we were awaiting the arrival of the *Endicott* I kept trying to console Ed, assuring him that he would be OK.

I went down to our quarters where I packed up what few personal items he had managed to keep. That didn't take long as about all we had were some shaving or toilet articles and a change of socks, most of which we had been given after we arrived at Odessa. Anyway, I got the stuff and brought it up to where he was and placed it on the stretcher with him. I remember the most cherished article he had was a long-sleeved white sweater and I had to pull the thing out of the sack to show him I had not forgotten it.

Ed Jurist is lowered into a motor launch to be taken to the destroyer USS Endicott *for medical treatment.*

The destroyer came alongside and shot a line over to our ship. The crewmen ran a cable across and the doctor came over on a breetches bouy. The sea was so rough Jurist had to be lowered into a motor launch for transport to the destroyer. They took him to a base hospital somewhere in the Azores.

I learned later that Jurist's injury was only a severe muscle strain. He was transferred from the *Endicott* to a hospital ship and wound up in Naples, Italy. He didn't arrive in the United States for about two months. Although Jurist and I kept in touch, this was the last time I would see him for about twenty years.

After transferring Jurist, the ship continued its voyage without further incident. I didn't offer to wrestle with anyone else. We landed in Newport News on May 7, 1945, just one day before the war ended in Europe.

FOR US THE WAR IS OVER

Although we were docked in the harbor we were not unloaded until the next day, May 8, and what a great feeling it was! Before we were unloaded we had heard from several sources that Germany had surrendered. Then the news was broadcast by the captain over the ship's loud speaker system. The whole ship seemed to explode with cheering and shouting! All over the harbor ships were blowing their horns, and bells were ringing all around the city. We were still onboard ship but I can imagine what a celebration there must have been on shore and downtown.

Once ashore we were given a royal reception at our barracks where we were to remain while we were processed and arrangements were made for us to be placed on furlough.

The first thing I—and most of us—did was to phone home. This was a moving experience—sad for some of the guys with "Dear John" letters or big family problems awaiting them but a great thrill for the majority of us. I know my family was happy and relieved to have at least one son safely home.

As soon as most of us had the chance to make our phone calls we were told to go to the mess hall where a big feast was prepared for us. The number-one choice of nearly every POW there was steak, along with all the trimmings. I wonder how many of us went to bed that night with stomach aches from stuffing ourselves. I know I did.

Our waiters were German POWs and they were really attentive. They must have been practicing their manners for I never saw any group of guys so anxious to please. Many of them would also be returning to their homes in the not-so-distant future—the United States began to release German POWs in May 1945. I know that a large number would have preferred to remain right where they were, here in the good old U.S. of A. Except for seeing their loved ones, they were heading for some pretty bleak times.

The German POWs knew we were returning ex-POWs and they were bumping heads to be of service to us. All of the attention we were getting plus the fact we had finally reached stateside was just about more than we could comprehend for a while. We were in Newport News for a few days and then we were issued furlough papers to go home for about three weeks.

They say you can't go home again. I literally couldn't. Home wasn't there anymore. The building and expansion of Del Valle Army Air Force Base—or Bergstrom Army Air Force Base as it had been renamed in March 1943—had pretty well disrupted the lives of the people in Del Valle. Little was left or recognizable of the thriving little community where I had grown up.

I returned to find my parents living in Austin. My father had given up his blacksmith shop and worked in town as a carpenter with Capitol City Furniture Company. My mother ran a rooming house at 4203 Guadalupe.

While I was on furlough I met Evelyn Jane Sims. Her sister, Louetta, had a room at Mom's rooming house. I suppose my mother had been telling her all about me and Louetta had relayed the stories to Evelyn. Evelyn and I started running around together immediately and it didn't take long for me to decide that she was the one for me.

What time I wasn't spending with Evelyn I was going around visiting other relatives and trying to eat myself to death on my mother's good home cooking. I still had weight to gain back, but it didn't take too long for me to overcome that problem.

At the end of my furlough I was ordered to report to the Rehabilitation Center in Miami, Florida. This was located in several of the real nice hotels there on the beach at Miami.

When I arrived in Miami I felt that my life had made a complete circle. Here I was back at the place that I last saw as I left the States for combat—I did it all, saw it all, and here I was back in Miami trying to make sense out of the whole ball of wax.

Once again I found myself in the good company of Bob Rector and Tex Reynolds. Except for our wrestling match, I suppose I would have had Ed Jurist there to share in our rehabilitation. He was still about two months from reaching the States.

Anyway, the first thing we did was to rent a car and start making the rounds of all the night clubs, bars, and any other places of entertainment we could find. The "big band" era was in full swing and everyone jitterbugged to songs like "String of Pearls" and "In the Mood." My favorite, of course, was "Don't Fence Me In."

We had been given a pretty good sum of back pay and we intended to waste as little time as possible spending it all. The high prices there in Miami were conducive to helping us with that chore. With our determined attitude we got rid of all our money in short order.

I became aware that there had been a heck of a lot of changes in the American economy since the last time I spent money here in the States. When I went in the service I was paying about twenty-five cents for a Coke in any bar and now soft drinks were up to $1.50 minimum.

As the French would say, *"C'est la guerre!"*

Anyway, we slogged our way through about thirty days of R&R—not too many lectures, although some of us could have benefited from a good strong lecture from our folks. One of the things I enjoyed, once I was stateside, was Bill Mauldin's cartoons in *Stars and Stripes*. Willie and Joe were just a couple of sad-sack GIs in the muddy foxholes of Italy and France but any serviceman could appreciate their humor.

I don't think it took long for us to get readjusted, and I know it didn't take long to separate us from most of the money we had accumulated during our time as POWs.

I suppose the most difficult thing for us to understand was that we were not paid for any of the time we were not in the control of the German authorities. It seemed like some kind of dirty joke to us. We had risked our lives to escape. We believed it was our duty. Then we were told we should have remained good little prisoners if we expected our government to pay us. Anyway, as with all the other incomprehensible things about the military, we could only shrug and go on about our way.

At least we were alive and home. We were grateful for that.

We remained in Miami for about a month. Then I was sent to Love Field in Dallas, Texas. Being stationed in Dallas gave me the opportunity to hitch-hike or catch a ride home once or twice a month and a chance to date Evelyn. I had hopes that she would begin to realize what a fine fellow I was deep down inside.

The Army had established Love Field before the first World War. The field operated as a civilian airport between the wars until it was reactivated in 1942. By the time I was assigned there, it was headquarters of the Fifth Ferrying Group, Air Transport Command.

I was given the task of flying a large number of old war-weary airplanes to Pyote Air Base near Monahans in Ward County in West Texas. P-51, B-29, and B-24 crews had trained there and at one time there had been a large compound of German POWs at Pyote.

Airmen stationed at Pyote called it the "Rattlesnake Bomber Base" for hundreds of very sound reasons. If you were smart you walked around looking down at your feet. The field had been built about the same time as the one at Del Valle, but by the time I got there not much was left of the base. Only a handful of personnel serviced it. It was a burial ground for beat-up old airplanes. The used-up airplanes were parked there, wing-tip to wing-tip as far as the eye could see, and left to dry rot in the desert climate.

I had anticipated being a little afraid to fly again but it really didn't seem to bother me. I asked to be reassigned to a B-29 Bomber school for flight engineers. At the time the war with Japan was not yet over and I thought I might get a chance to fly with a bomber group in the Pacific Theater.

One of the planes later abandoned for a time at Pyote was the "Enola Gay." The B-29 Superfortress bomber had been especially adapted to carry the atomic bomb dropped on Hiroshima, Japan on August 6, 1945. The bombing of Hiroshima and of Nagasaki three days later was followed by Japan's surrender on August 15.

With the war finally over and before I had completed my course of training, the Air Force started discharging people under the point system. I was sent to Randolph Field in San Antonio, Texas for separation. On November 19, 1945 I was given an Honorable Discharge from the U.S. Army Air Force with the rank of Technical Sergeant. My chest wasn't sagging from the weight of the medals I had won, but I was very proud of my Good Conduct Medal. On that one, I had a strong hunch that the German High Command would have protested had they been offered the chance.

(Photo by Deborah Ledesman)

The author, Harvey E. Gann, exchanged his Aerial Gunner's Wings for a Prisoner of War medal.

AFTERWORD

At the time of my discharge I had become very bitter.

I wanted nothing more to do with the service or any part thereof. I was easily angered when my civilian friends talked about the rationing and scarcities and hardships they had endured while the war was going on. Many times I simply walked away to avoid losing my temper and becoming hostile. In my opinion, they knew nothing of hardship.

I am happy to say my negative feelings lasted only a short time. I soon adjusted to my freedom and new surroundings.

My brother, Willard, was also back from service. He'd been in the Navy, attached to the Marine Corps as a medic in the South Pacific. Willard and I were always very close and we spent a great deal of time together, talking about all the things we had seen and about the war in general.

We were both deeply sympathetic to the people, both military and civilians, who had been held as prisoners by the Japanese. The Germans at least had made a reciprocal effort to observe the Geneva Convention. But

Harvey (left) and his younger brother, Fred Willard, had a lot to talk about when they returned home after World War II. Willard had been in the Navy, attached to the Marine Corps as a medic in the South Pacific.

the Japanese had never ratified the agreement and did not feel obligated to provide humane treatment for their prisoners. Many died of diseases, exposure, and starvation.

I know that my mother was very happy to have us both back home, safe and sound. I can only guess at the heartache and despair she and all the other mothers across the world must have endured.

At first I just messed around, trying to get the chip off my shoulder. Some people had been more fortunate than I was during the war but I couldn't go around blaming them for their good fortune—nor for my own POW experiences. I began hearing and reading of much worse stories than mine from men and women who'd been prisoners of war in Japan. I struggled to put things into some kind of balance.

I suppose one thing continued to nag at me: Why was I the only survivor of my ten-man crew? For what purpose had I been permitted to live?

With the passing years I have more or less given up trying to solve that puzzle. I've decided to be content with the fact that I am still here on Earth and that should be good enough.

After a few months I was tired of loafing and playing around. I went to work for a construction company. At the same time I applied for a position with the Austin Police Department.

During World War II, with most young, able-bodied men in the service or in essential industries, police departments across the country had to make do with older men, some with physical impairments. Police departments were eager to hire returning veterans and take advantage of our training and experience.

One day while I was on the construction site a couple of men from APD came out and told me I'd been accepted.

On March 29, 1946 I joined the ranks of "Austin's Finest" as a probationary patrolman. R.C. (Bob) Miles, who later became Chief of Police, entered the department at the same time I did. For about a month I was in a patrol car but always with another officer. Then I attended the department's first Austin Police Academy. My certificate, dated September 6, 1946, is signed by Russell Forester, director of education, and Police Chief R. D. (Boss) Thorp.

The girl I'd met while I was on furlough—Evelyn Sims—and I had liked each other right away. We started

Harvey Gann and the strikingly attractive brunette, Evelyn Sims, began dating after Gann's return from Germany.

dating seriously. She was attractive, intelligent, and had a great sense of humor. With the security of a job in the police department I finally got the courage to ask her to marry me.

We married October 12, 1946. I never have any trouble remembering our wedding anniversary. I always say on that date Columbus discovered a new world and so did I. We lived with my folks for a few months and then for a short period with Evelyn's parents. This gave us a chance to save enough money to buy a house under the GI Bill and we moved into our own place. I guess there must have been thousands of veterans all over the country doing the same thing. I am sure many of them must have been looking back and wondering how they had lived to have this come about. I know I was, for one!

I was still bitter about the fact that my Army Air Force pay had stopped every time I escaped. Even if I'd known that at the time I would have broken out anyway. No one, not even the United States government, could have paid me enough money to stay in those prison camps.

I finally did get some government money—back pay or food allowance or severance, I don't remember. I do remember the amount was small but it was enough for me to take Evelyn to an appliance store on South Congress Avenue and buy an electric sewing machine for her. She made lots of clothes with it, especially later as our children came along. On a police patrolman's pay that really helped us.

In 1953 the movie *Stalag 17*, starring William Holden, came out. The plot hinged on prisoner of war escape attempts. I had mixed feelings about going to see it. I'd had eight years to heal, but had that been enough? The movie was based on the Broadway play written by Donald Bevan and Edmund Trzcinski—ex-GIs and both former prisoners of Germany, so I imagine the play was true to their own experiences.

The movie had been dramatized for box office appeal. Still, parts of it were realistic enough to bring back a flood of memories—some of them very painful.

Evelyn and I saw the movie together. I am not sure she got to enjoy it very much because of my constant stream of remarks. She knew what my experiences and problems were and she let me get whatever I wanted to off my chest.

By the time "Hogan's Heroes," the television situation comedy starring Bob Crane, came out in 1965

I could laugh at it. The plots bore no resemblance to the truth and I enjoyed watching the bumbling Sergeant Schulze and the well-intentioned Colonel Klink, who always seemed to be caught in the middle between the innocent, prank-loving POWs and the evil Gestapo. I only wish our guards in real life had been half so stupid. My escapes would have been much easier. I would have been home much sooner.

I suppose I would have to say most war movies or prisoner of war programs are about as realistic as most cop shows—which is to say, not very.

A funny coincidence happened in 1961—if I'd seen it on TV I wouldn't have believed it could happen in real life.

I'd been promoted to lieutenant and was head of the APD vice detail. Acting on a tip about illegal gambling, I led a raid on a building in East Austin. Sure enough, we caught seven men in the middle of a poker game— and one of them was my old buddy, Tex Reynolds from Jacksboro by way of *Stalag Luft* IV.

The situation was awkward. I mumbled something like, "Say, Tex, it's great to see you again! How've you been? Sorry, but I'm going to have to take you in."

A happier coincidence occurred in 1970, while I was a captain with the APD. I was attending a narcotics law enforcement conference in Laredo, down on the Texas-Mexico border, when I got a long distance telephone call. I couldn't imagine who was calling me because only my family and my department knew where I was. My first thought was something bad had happened.

"Is this the Harvey Gann who used to be a POW?" the voice asked.

When the brief conversation ended I left Laredo as soon as I could and headed to Harlingen, 165 miles

The author (left) enjoyed a brief reunion with Ed Jurist in September 1970.

away, for an unexpected reunion with my old buddy, Ed Jurist.

Jurist, then a colonel with the Confederate Air Force, had flown into Harlingen on CAF business. He had mentioned that he had a friend "somewhere in Texas" and asked for help in tracking me down—and between military and police authorities, he found me. An account in the September 27, 1970 issue of the *Valley Morning Star* (Harlingen) said our reunion was "enthusiastic, loud and joyful." It was all of that and more.

Evelyn worked for Southwestern Bell until our first child was born. We have two beautiful daughters. Our older, Sandra Lynette Allen, has four children and lives in Seattle. The younger, Deborah Jane Ledesma, joined the Austin Police Department in 1979 and is now a sergeant.

Eventually Evelyn and I were able to visit Germany. I had no desire to locate or visit the sites of the *Stalags* but we enjoyed the tours and the friendly people we met. I felt my healing was at last complete.

I retired December 30, 1983 after almost thirty-eight years with the Austin Police Department. I had risen through the ranks from patrolman to detective, lieutenant, captain, and finally major. Most of those years I was in charge of the vice and narcotic detail.

But that is another war and another story.

-30-

Harvey Gann retired from the Austin Police Department with the rank of major. He and his wife Evelyn enjoy a number of leisure activities, including square dancing.

Harvey E. Gann (center), the author of Escape I Must!, received his Prisoner of War medal in a ceremony at Bergstrom Air Force Base (formerly Del Valle Air Base.)

CHRONOLOGY

Author's note: Few of us men and women who were actively engaged in World War II had any but the faintest idea what was happening outside our own units—and no idea at all about other fronts and other theaters. This list of dates, far from complete, is provided to help you put my story into context with your own.

September 1, 1939 — German troops began their advance into Poland.

September 3, 1939 — Britain, France, Australia and New Zealand declared war on Germany.

September 17, 1939 — Soviets moved into Poland.

September 29, 1939 — Soviets and Germany signed a Friendship Treaty.

May 24, 1940 — German forces surrounded Dunkirk in northern France.

May 26, 1940 — Evacuation of Dunkirk began. Nearly 340,000 Allied troops escaped.

June 10, 1940 — Italy declared war on Britain and France.

June 22, 1940 — France signed an armistice with Germany.

September 7, 1940 — Blitz on London began.

November 11, 1940 — Britain attacked the Italian fleet at Taranto.

August 5, 1941 — Siege of Odessa began and lasted seventy-three days.

June 22, 1941 — Germany invaded U.S.S.R.

October 19, 1941 — Moscow was under siege by the Germans.

December 7, 1941 — Japanese bombers attacked Pearl Harbor.

December 8, 1941 — President Roosevelt delivered a war message to Congress.

December 11, 1941 — Germany and Italy declared war on the U.S.

September 14, 1942 — I received my induction notice.

September 19, 1942 — Del Valle Air Base was officially activated.

October 7, 1942 — The Allies established the War Crimes Commission.

May 1, 1943 — The 449th Heavy Bombardment Group was activated at Tucson, Arizona.

September 9, 1943 — U.S. Fifth Army began landing south of Salerno.

September 10, 1943 — Dulag Luft was moved near the center of Frankfurt's residential section about 1,600 yards from the main railroad yards. This was a violation of Article 9 of the Geneva Convention.

September 27, 1943 — Foggia airfields in Italy were abandoned by the Germans.

December 14, 1943 — Our ten-man crew left Miami in our assigned B-24. On this same day, the Russians launched their winter offensive.

January 7, 1944 — We landed at Grottaglie, Italy—home to the 449th Bombardment Squadron of the Fifteenth Air Wing.

January 22, 1944 — U.S. Fifth Army began an assault on Anzio beachhead.

January 30, 1944 — U.S. Fifteenth Air Force planes attacked German air facilities at Udine in northern Italy. Our crew's last mission, from which only I would return.

On this same day, U.S. Rangers on Anzio beachhead were ambushed and two battalions almost entirely eliminated.

January 31, 1944 — B-17s and B-24s, escorted by P-38s and P-47s, again bombed Udine.

February 18, 1944 — I arrived at Stalag Luft VI. On this same day, the Germans made a deep penetration into the Anzio beachhead against the U.S. 179th Infantry Regiment.

February 22, 1944 — U.S. Fifteenth Air Force bombers from Italy joined in bombing attacks on German aircraft factories.

February 25, 1944 — U.S. Fifteenth Air Force attacked the Regensburg aircraft factory. The Fifteenth lost about twenty percent of its bombers.

March 11, 1944 — My first escape from Stalag Luft VI, with LaMarca, Routon and Stapleton.

March 18, 1944 — We were recaptured after a week of freedom. On this same day, the RAF dropped 3,000 tons of bombs on Frankfurt. This raid was followed by another on March 22. The raids on Frankfurt destroyed Dulag Luft.

March 28, 1944 — We were taken from the Tilsit jail.

April 2, 1944 — The Fifteenth Air Force attacked Steyr, Austria, with nearly 500 Flying Fortresses and Liberators.

April 9, 1944 — Easter Sunday. LaMarca, Routon, Stapleton and I were recaptured by the Germans near Pillau. On this same day, Russia launched the final drive to oust the Germans from the Crimea.

In the Pacific Theater, the British 14th Army was surrounded at Kohima by the Japanese.

April 26, 1944 — Verona, Italy fell to the Allies.

May 12, 1944 — Stalag Luft IV opened to American prisoners.

May 30, 1944 — We escapees were brought from Königsberg and placed in the stockade for fourteen days of solitary confinement at Stalag Luft VI.

June 4, 1944 — U. S. Fifth Army entered Rome.

June 6, 1944 — D-Day. The Allied invasion of Normandy began.

June 13, 1944 — We escapees were removed from the stockade and returned to our barracks at Stalag Luft VI.

July 15, 1944 — Large number of prisoners were removed from Stalag Luft VI.

July 17, 1944 — Russian forces swept into Poland.

July 18, 1944 — The "Run Up the Road" from Kiefheide to Stalag Luft IV.

July 19, 1944 — Five German divisions were trapped in the Ukraine.

July 20, 1944 — German officers made an attempt on Hitler's life.

July 31, 1944 — Russian troops reached positions ten miles from Warsaw.

September 12, 1944 — British bombers dropped 400,000 incendiary bombs on Frankfurt am Main.

October 10, 1944 — Russian troops reached the Baltic Sea near Memel, Lithuania.

January 9, 1945 — U.S. Sixth Army landed in Lingayen Gulf in Luzon.

February 6, 1945 — The Black March.

February 10, 1945 — Jurist, Rector, Reynolds and I escaped from a barn where we were being held by the Germans.

February 13, 1945 — British bombers raided Dresden, followed the next day by American bombers.

February 19, 1945 — American Marines landed on the island of Iwo Jima in the Pacific and raised the American flag.

March 1, 1945 — MacArthur returned to Corregidor.

March 7, 1945 — German bombers resumed bombing of Britain.

April 2, 1945 — Russian forces were within fifty miles of Berlin.

April 3, 1945 — We arrived in Odessa and were met by the American Military Mission.

April 12, 1945 — President Franklin Roosevelt died. Harry Truman became the thirty-third president.

April 18, 1945 — Ernie Pyle, popular war correspondent, was killed by a sniper on Okinawa.

April 28, 1945 — Benito Mussolini was shot and killed by Italian partisans.

April 30, 1945 — Hitler committed suicide.

May 7, 1945 — We liberated POWs landed in Newport News, Virginia.

May 8, 1945 — The war ended in Europe.

May 10, 1945 — The last German forces in Czechoslovakia surrendered.

July 29, 1945 — The American cruiser U.S.S. *Indianapolis* was torpedoed and sunk in the Pacific, with the loss of 883 men.

August 6, 1945 — An American B-29 bomber, the "Enola Gay," dropped the first atomic bomb on Hiroshima.

August 11, 1945 — An American bomber dropped an atomic bomb on Nagasaki, Japan.

August 15, 1945 — Japan surrendered.

September 2, 1945 — Japan surrendered formally in a ceremony aboard the U.S.S. *Missouri*.

November 19, 1945 — I was honorably discharged from the United States Army Air Force.

GLOSSARY

ack-ack — anti-aircraft fire.

B-24 Liberator — four-engine, twin-tail heavy bomber. Ugly on the ground but graceful in the air.

bail-out rations — a small packet of emergency rations.

bandits — enemy aircraft.

bomb bay — portion of the fuselage in an airplane where the bombs are lodged.

Brenner Pass — Alpine pass connecting Italy with Austria.

chute-shock — jolt experienced when the open parachute fully catches the air.

D-Bar — A special nutritional chocolate bar for emergencies.

Dakar — capital of French West Africa.

Davis-Monthan — air base near Tucson, Arizona.

Dulag — short for *Durchgangslager,* a transit camp.

Dulag Luft — airmen's transit camp.

eighty-eights — German 88-mm artillery pieces, first used as anti-aircraft later against tanks. Fired 22-pound shells with deadly accuracy.

ersatz — German word for substitute or synthetic.

feather the engine — to rotate the airplane's propeller blades to an angle at which they produce minimum drag.

ferrets — one of the Kriegies' pet names for German guards.

fire stop — sometimes called fire interrupter; automatically stops fire of an aircraft's moving guns so as to avoid hitting any part of the aircraft.

Fortaleza — large port in northeast Brazil.

Geneva Convention — ninety-seven specific articles protecting the rights of prisoners of war. The Convention called for humane treatment, information about prisoners, and visits to the camps by protecting powers.

Gestapo — Nazi secret police organization.

goons — German prison guards.

Grottaglie — small Italian village and site of Allied bomber base.

gunner's turret — revolving light metal framework and Plexiglas enclosure.

Hauptmann — German military title: captain.

honey-wagon — detail assigned to clean or empty latrines.

Kilroy was here — favorite slogan of the American GIs. The words mysteriously appeared on latrines, phone booths, walls, street signs, overpasses, and water towers.

Kriegies — American POWs' name for themselves. Short for *Kriegsgefangene*.

Lager — German for camp.

Lili Marlene — German war song that became a favorite of Americans and British as well.

Lindbergh, Charles — American aviator, first to fly solo across the Atlantic. An advocate of neutrality, he refused a commission but flew as a volunteer civilian.

Luftlager — German camp for captured airmen.

Luftwaffe — German Air Force.

Mae West — inflatable rubber flotation device for airmen forced to bail out over water.

Man of Confidence — noncommissioned officer chosen in each *Stalag* to deal with the camp's commandant and to relay orders and information to the POWs.

mission — an ordered operation against the enemy.

Memel — East Prussian seaport given to Lithuania after World War I; reclaimed by the Germans in 1939.

Messerschmitt Me-109 — one-seat German fighter plane.

Mosquito — British-built de Haviland two-seat night-fighter.

Norden bombsight — a precision optical device that helped keep bombers straight and steady during a bomb run.

Odessa — important Ukrainian port and naval base on the Black Sea.

P-38 Lightning — U.S. twin-engine, single-seat fighter plane. The Germans called it "fork-tailed devil."

peel off — to curve away from another aircraft.

protecting power — a neutral nation, such as Sweden or Switzerland, helping to oversee the humane treatment of POWs under the Geneva Convention.

Quonset — a prefabricated shelter with a semicircular roof of corrugated metal. Used for barracks, offices, and storage.

reader — sometimes called a reporter. A POW who relayed news orally from barracks to barracks.

SS — the Black Shirts, organized by Hitler to protect Nazi party interests.

Scharnhorst — German battle cruiser, pride of the German navy with its nine sixteen-inch guns. Sunk while attempting to intercept an Allied convoy.

Stalag — short for *Stammlager*, a permanent German army camp.

strafed — machine-gunned.

Taranto — major Italian port on the Mediterranean Sea, captured by the Allies in September 1943.

Terror Flieger — a terrorist airman, so called because the Germans believed airmen had special training as commandos and saboteurs.

tush hog — a mean, aggressive person; a fighter.

Twining, Nathan F. — commanding general of the Fifteenth Air Force in Italy in 1944-45.

Udine — industrial town on east end of north Italian plain.

U.S.O. — United Service Organizations helped provide social and recreational entertainment for American service men.

WAAF — Women's Auxiliary Air Force. Volunteer women pilots who flew tow-planes and ferried airplanes overseas.

Wehrmacht — German armed forces or military power.

Willow Run — Ford plant near Detroit. During WWII, converted from automobiles to B-24 assembly line.

wingman — second man in a team of two planes. Flies his plane to one side and just behind the leader. Job is to protect the leader.

Publisher's note: Woodburner Press gratefully acknowledges the following:

Margret Hofmann, for correcting the colloquial German and proofreading the final manuscript. Helmut and Barbara Hartmann, for helping Ms. Hofmann recall a version of "Lili Marlene."

Dr. Michael Katz, for correcting the transliterated Russian words and identifying the Russian song, "Moscow Nights."

Colonel Charles M. Lowe, for assistance in preparing the Glossary.

INDEX

Postscript

When this manuscript was nearly ready for publication I tried to find out more about Colonel Darr H. Alkire. I learned that he had gone down the very next day—January 31, 1944—after my ill-fated mission to Udine, Italy. I'm now certain I saw him in *Dulag Luft* at Frankfurt am Main. I learned that he became the Senior American Officer at *Stalag Luft* III. His firm determination dealing with the camp officials spared his men some of the forced marches and other inhumane treatment.

While I was seeking information about Colonel Alkire, Harry E. May, squadron line chief of the 718th Squadron, told me that I was not the sole survivor of my crew. There had been others. I was stunned! I couldn't believe that any of my fellow crew members could have bailed out of our burning ship before it exploded. If they had survived, surely I would have heard about it from other POWs who were captured at about the same time I was.

In an effort to find out more, I telephoned Richard F. Downey, Lieutenant Colonel, U.S. Air Force (Retired), who is secretary of the 449th Bombardment Group Association. His records seemed to confirm my original belief—there had been no other survivors from our B-24. But he added that there *might* have been survivors, POWs who had not sent their names into the association.

So the matter remains controversial. If any readers have information about any of the men mentioned in my account, I will appreciate hearing from you.

Harvey E. Gann
18202 Travis Drive
Lago Vista, TX 78645

ADDENDUM

Only a few days after the publication of my book, I received thru the mail a list of 449th Bomb Group members who were buried in the American Cemetery in Florence, Italy. It is with a saddened heart that I must now confirm that my entire crew was lost in the explosion of our plane over Udine, Italy on January 30, 1944. There in bold print were the names of my crew members with the exception of Fletcher Porter, my co-pilot, whose body had been returned to the states for burial. Now, there was no doubt as to their fate. Although I had always felt certain of their death, I had kept hope in my heart after my conversations with other bomb group members who thought some of my crew might have survived.

Since the publication of Escape I Must?, my wife Evelyn and I have visited Italy two times with the 449th Bomb Group and with Col. Lee Kenny as our tour leader. On both occasions we had the opportunity to visit our old air base at Grottaglie and many of the cities that we had bombed during the war. On our tour this past year, Sept. 3-17, 2001, we enjoyed the company of Charles A. LaMarca, my ole escapee buddy from Stalag Luft VI at Hydekrug. Our tour group visited the Military Cemetery in Florence. LaMarca and I read the names of our crew members inscribed on the Memorial Wall and had Evelyn take our picture at the grave of our pilot, Ben Kendall. Kendall was the only member recovered besides that of Porter, whose body I saw pulled from the waters of the Adriatic Sea at the time of my capture.

With the exception of Sept. 11th the tour was a great experience and the outpouring of sympathy from the Italian people concerning the terrorist act brought tears to the eyes of many in our group. To round out this story, I have had the pleasure of hearing from Jake Rowton's son Dale and his wife Verita. I learned that Jake had passed away several years back, leaving a fine family with fond memories of him. Hopefully, and if time doesn't run out on me, I could still have a chance to meet them.

C'est La Guerre
Harvey E. Gann
18202 Travis Drive
Lago Vista, TX 78645

AMERICAN
MILITARY CEMETERY
Florence, Italy
Gann and LaMarca
at
Memorial Wall

AMERICAN
MILITARY CEMETERY
Florence, Italy
Gann and LaMarca
at grave of
pilot Ben Kendall